ABIDE
IN THE
SECRET
PLACE

A BIDE
IN THE
SECRET
PLACE

ANDREW MURRAY

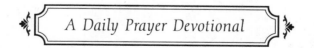

A Daily Prayer Devotional

WHITAKER
HOUSE

This book contains excerpts from *God's Best Secrets*, © 1998 by Whitaker House. The text of this book has been updated for the modern reader. Words, expressions, and sentence structure have been revised for clarity and readability.

ABIDE IN THE SECRET PLACE
A Daily Prayer Devotional

ISBN: 978-1-64123-513-6
eBook ISBN: 978-1-64123-514-3
Printed in the United States of America
© 2020 by Whitaker House

Whitaker House
1030 Hunt Valley Circle
New Kensington, PA 15068
www.whitakerhouse.com

Library of Congress Control Number: 2020945834

2 3 4 5 6 7 8 9 10 11 **UI** 27 26 25 24 23 22

CONTENTS

1

FROM DAY TO DAY

The inward man is being renewed day by day.
—2 Corinthians 4:16

There is one lesson that all young Christians should learn, and that is the absolute necessity of fellowship with Jesus each day. This lesson is not always taught at the beginning of the Christian life, nor is it always understood by the young convert. He should realize that the grace he has received—the forgiveness of his sins, his acceptance as God's child, and his joy in the Holy Spirit—can only be preserved by daily renewal in fellowship with Jesus Christ Himself.

Many Christians backslide because this truth is not clearly taught. They are unable to stand against the temptations of the world and of their old nature. They strive to do their best to fight against sin and to serve God, but they have no strength. They have never really grasped the secret that the Lord Jesus in heaven will continue His work in them every day, but only on one condition: every soul must give Him time each day to impart His love and His grace. Time alone with the Lord Jesus each day is the indispensable condition of growth and power.

Read Matthew 11:25–30. Christ says, *"Come to Me…and I will give you rest.…Learn from Me…and you will find rest for your souls"* (vv. 28–29). The Lord will teach us just how meek and humble He is. Bow before Him, tell Him that you long for Him and His love, and He will let His love rest on you. This is a thought not only for young Christians, but also for all who love the Lord.

If you desire to live this life of fellowship with Christ, if you wish to enjoy this blessed experience each day, then learn the lesson of spending time each day, without exception, in fellowship with your Lord. In this way, your inner man will be renewed from day to day.

2

JESUS

You shall call His name JESUS,
for He will save His people from their sins.
—Matthew 1:21

Because the Lord Jesus was a person, He had His own individual name. His mother, His disciples, and all His friends called Him by this name, Jesus. But they probably thought little of what that name meant. And the majority of Christians today hardly know what a treasure is contained in that name, Jesus: *"He will save His people from their sins."*

Many think of His death on the cross or of His work in heaven as our Intercessor, but they do not realize that Jesus is a living person in heaven who thinks of us each day and longs to reveal Himself. He desires us to bring Him our love and adoration each day.

Christians pray to Christ to save them from their sins, but they know very little how the blessed work is done. The living Christ reveals Himself to us, and through the power of His love, the love of sin is expelled. It is through personal fellowship with Him that Jesus saves us from our sins. I must come as an individual, with my heart and all the sin that is in it, to Jesus as an almighty personal Savior in whom God's holiness dwells. And as He and I commune together in the expression of mutual love and desire, by the work of His Holy Spirit in my heart, His love will expel and conquer all the sin.

Oh Christian, you will find the secret of happiness and holiness in fellowship with Jesus each day. Your heart will long for the hour of prayer as the best hour of the day. As you learn to take time to be alone with Him each day, you will experience His presence, enabling you to love Him, to serve Him, and to walk in His ways throughout the day. Through this unbroken fellowship, you will learn the secret of the power of a truly godly life.

3

THE INNER CHAMBER

When thou prayest, enter into thine inner chamber, and having shut thy door, pray to thy Father which is in secret, and thy Father which seeth in secret shall recompense thee.
—Matthew 6:6 RV

Have you ever thought what a wonderful privilege it is that everyone each day, and each hour of the day, has the liberty of asking God to meet him in the inner chamber and to hear what he has to say? We imagine that every Christian uses such a privilege gladly and faithfully. But how many really do take advantage of the privilege?

"*When thou prayest,*" said Jesus, "*enter into thine inner chamber, and having shut thy door, pray to thy Father which is in secret.*" This means two things. First, shut the world out, and withdraw from all worldly thoughts and activities. Second, shut yourself in alone with God, to pray to Him in secret. Let this be your chief aim in prayer: to realize the presence of your heavenly Father. Let your watchword be, "Alone with God."

This is only the beginning. As you take time to realize His presence with you and to pray to *"thy Father which seeth in secret,"* you can do so in the full assurance that He knows how you long for His help and guidance, and that He will incline His ear to you.

Then follows the great promise: *"Thy Father which seeth in secret shall recompense thee."* The Father will see to it that your prayer is not in vain. All through the activities of a busy day, the answer to your prayer will be granted. Prayer in secret will be followed by the secret working of God in your heart.

The Lord Jesus has given us the promise of His presence, and He shows us the way to the inner chamber. Therefore, He will surely be with us to teach us to pray. It is through Him that we have access to the Father. (See John 14:6.) Be childlike and trustful in your fellowship with Christ. Confess each sin; bring your every need. Offer your prayer to the Father in the name of Christ. Prayer in fellowship with Jesus cannot be in vain.

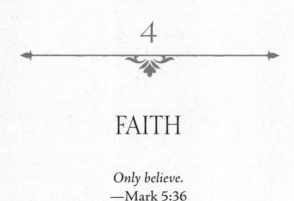

4

FAITH

Only believe.
—Mark 5:36

We have here a lesson of the greatest importance. When we are alone in the inner chamber, we must send up our petitions, trusting implicitly in the love of God and in the power of the Lord Jesus. Take time to ask yourself the question, Is my heart full of a great and steadfast faith in God's love? If this is not the case, do not begin to pray just yet. Faith does not come of itself.

Consider quietly how impossible it is for God to lie. He is ready with infinite love to give you a blessing (Psalm 29:11). Take some passage of Scripture in which God's power, faithfulness, and love are revealed. Take hold of the words and say, "Yes, Lord, I will pray in firm faith in You and in Your great love."

It is a mistake to limit the word *faith* to the forgiveness of sins and to our acceptance as children of God. Faith includes far more than this. We must have faith in all that God is willing to do for us. We must have faith each day according to our special needs. God is infinitely great and powerful, and Christ has so much grace for each new day, that our faith must reach out afresh each day according to the need of the day.

When you enter into the inner chamber, even before you begin to pray, ask yourself, Do I really believe that God is here with me and that the Lord Jesus will help me to pray? Do I believe that I can expect to spend a blessed time in communion with my God?

Jesus often taught His disciples how indispensable faith was to true prayer. He will teach you this lesson, too. Remain in fellowship with Him, and ask Him to strengthen your faith in His almighty power. Christ says to you and to me, as He did to Martha, *"Did I not say to you that if you would believe you would see the glory of God?"* (John 11:40).

5

THE WORD OF GOD

Man shall not live by bread alone, but by every word that
proceeds from the mouth of God.
—Matthew 4:4

In the above verse, our Lord compared the Word of God to our daily bread, thereby teaching us a great lesson. Bread is indispensable to life. We all understand this. However strong a person may be, if he takes no nourishment, he will grow weaker, and he will die. If an illness prevents me from eating, I will die. It is the same with the Word of God. The Word contains a heavenly principle and works powerfully in those who believe.

Bread must be eaten. I may know all about bread. I may have bread and give it to others. I may have bread in my house and on my table in great abundance, but that will not help me unless I eat it. Similarly, a mere knowledge of God's Word and even the preaching of it to others will not benefit me. It is not enough to think about it. Rather, I must feed on God's Word and take it into my heart and life. In love and obedience I must take hold of the words of God and let them take full possession of my heart. Then they will indeed be words of life.

Bread must be eaten daily, and the same is true of God's Word. The psalmist wrote, "*Blessed is the man…[whose] delight is in the law of the LORD, and in His law he meditates day and night*" (Psalm 1:1–2); "*Oh, how I love Your law! It is my meditation all the day*"

(Psalm 119:97). To secure a strong and powerful spiritual life, an intake of God's Word every day is indispensable.

When He was on earth, the Lord Jesus learned, loved, and obeyed the Word of the Father. If you seek fellowship with Him, you will find Him in His Word. Christ will teach you to commune with the Father through the Word, just as He did on earth. You will learn, like Him, to live solely for the glory of God and the fulfillment of His Word.

6

HOW TO READ GOD'S WORD

Blessed is the man…[whose] delight is in the law of the
Lord, *and in His law he meditates day and night.*
—Psalm 1:1–2

Here are some simple rules for Bible reading. First, read God's Word with great reverence. Meditate a moment in silence on the thought that the words come from God Himself. Bow in deep reverence. Be silent before God. Let Him reveal His Word in your heart.

Second, read with careful attention. If you read the words carelessly, thinking that you can grasp their meaning with your human understanding, you will use the words superficially and will not enter into their depths. When someone tries to explain anything wonderful or beautiful to us, we give our entire attention to try to understand what is said. How much higher and deeper are God's thoughts than our thoughts! *"For as the heavens are higher than the earth, so are...My thoughts than your thoughts"* (Isaiah 55:9). We need to give our undivided attention to understand even the superficial meaning of the words. How much harder it is to grasp the spiritual meaning!

Next, read with the expectation of the guidance of God's Spirit. It is God's Spirit alone that can make the Word a living power in our hearts and lives. Read Psalm 119. Notice how earnestly David prayed that God would teach him, open his eyes, give him understanding, and incline his heart to God's ways. As you read, remember that God's Word and God's Spirit are inseparable.

Finally, read with the firm purpose of keeping the Word day and night in your heart and in your life. The whole heart and the whole life must come under the influence of the Word. David said, *"Oh, how I love Your law! It is my meditation all the day"* (Psalm 119:97). In the same manner, in the midst of his daily work, the believer can cherish God's Word in his heart and meditate on it. Read Psalm 119 again, until you accept God's Word with all your heart. Pray that God may teach you to understand it and to carry out its precepts in your life.

7

THE WORD AND PRAYER

Revive me, O Lord, according to Your word.
—Psalm 119:107

Prayer and the Word of God are inseparable and should always go together in the quiet time of the inner chamber. In His Word, God speaks to me; in prayer, I speak to God. If there is to be true fellowship, God and I must both take part. If I simply pray without using God's Word, I am apt to use my own words and thoughts. To really give prayer its power, I must take God's thoughts from His Word and present them before Him. Then I am enabled to pray according to God's Word. How indispensable God's Word is for all true prayer!

When you pray, you must seek to know God correctly. It is through the Word that the Holy Spirit gives you right thoughts of Him. The Word will also teach you how wretched and sinful you are. It reveals to you all the wonders that God will do for you and the strength He will give you to do His will. The Word teaches you how to pray with strong desire, with firm faith, and with constant perseverance. The Word teaches you not only what you are, but also what you may become through God's grace. Above all, it reminds you each day that Christ is the great Intercessor, and allows you to pray in His name.

Oh Christian, learn this great lesson, to renew your strength each day in God's Word, and thereby pray according to His will.

Now let us turn to the other side: prayer. We need prayer when we read God's Word: prayer to be taught by God to understand His Word, prayer that through the Holy Spirit we may rightly know and use God's Word, prayer that we may see in the Word that Christ is all in all, and will be all in us.

Blessed inner chamber, where I may approach God in Christ through the Word and prayer! There I may offer myself to God and His service, and be strengthened by the Holy Spirit, so that His love may be poured out in my heart (Romans 5:5), and I may daily walk in that love.

8

OBEDIENCE

Obey My voice…and I will be your God.
—Jeremiah 11:4

God gave this command to Israel when He gave them the law. But Israel had no power to keep the law. So God gave them a new covenant, to enable His people to live a life of obedience. We read, *"I will put My law in their minds, and write it on their hearts"* (Jeremiah 31:33); *"I will put My fear in their hearts so that they will not depart from Me"* (Jeremiah 32:40); *"I will…cause you to walk in My statutes"* (Ezekiel 36:27). These wonderful promises gave Israel the assurance that obedience would be their delight.

See what the Lord Jesus said about obedience: *"He who has My commandments and keeps them, it is he who loves Me"* (John 14:21); *"If anyone loves Me, he will keep My word; and My Father will love him, and We will come to him and make Our home with him"* (v. 23); *"If you keep My commandments, you will abide in My love"* (John 15:10). These words are an inexhaustible treasure. Through faith we can firmly trust Christ to enable us to live such a life of love and obedience.

No father can train his children unless they are obedient. No teacher can teach a child who continues to disobey him. No general can lead his soldiers to victory without prompt obedience. Pray that God will imprint this lesson on your heart: the life of faith is a life of obedience. As Christ lived in obedience to the Father, so we, too, need obedience for a life in the love of God.

But so many people think, "I cannot be obedient; it is impossible." Yes, impossible to you, but not to God. He has promised to *"cause you to walk in [His] statutes"* (Ezekiel 36:27). Pray and meditate on these words, and the Holy Spirit will enlighten your eyes, so that you will have power to do God's will. Let your fellowship with the Father and with the Lord Jesus Christ have this as its one aim: a life of quiet, determined, unquestioning obedience.

9

CONFESSION OF SIN

If we confess our sins, He is faithful and just to forgive us our sins and to cleanse us from all unrighteousness.
—1 John 1:9

Too often the confession of sin is superficial, and often it is quite neglected. Few Christians realize how necessary it is to be sincere about the matter. Some do not feel that an honest confession of sin gives power to live the life of victory over sin. But we, in fellowship with the Lord Jesus, need to confess with a sincere heart every sin that may be a hindrance in our Christian lives.

Read what David said: *"I acknowledged my sin to You....I said, 'I will confess my transgressions to the Lord,' and You forgave the iniquity of my sin....You are my hiding place...You shall surround me with songs of deliverance"* (Psalm 32:5, 7). David spoke of a time when he was unwilling to confess his sin. *"When I kept silent...Your hand was heavy upon me"* (vv. 3–4). But when he had confessed his sin, a wonderful change came.

Confession means not only that you confess your sin with shame, but also that you hand it over to God, trusting Him to take it away. Such a confession implies that you are wholly unable to get rid of your guilt, but by an act of faith you depend on God to deliver you. This deliverance means, in the first place, that you know your sins are forgiven, and secondly, that Christ undertakes to cleanse you from the sin and keep you from its power.

Oh Christian, if you are seeking to have fellowship with Jesus, do not fear to confess each sin in the confident assurance that there is deliverance. Let there be a mutual understanding between the Lord Jesus and yourself that you will confess each sin and will obtain forgiveness. Then you will know your Lord as Jesus, who saves His people from their sins (Matthew 1:21). Believe that there is great power in the confession of sin, for the burden of sin was borne by our Lord and Savior.

10

THE FIRST LOVE

Nevertheless I have this against you,
that you have left your first love.
—Revelation 2:4

In the verses preceding Revelation 2:4, eight signs are mentioned that show the zeal and activity of the church at Ephesus. But there was one bad sign, and the Lord said, *"I will come to you quickly and remove your lampstand from its place; unless you repent"* (v. 5). And what was this sign? *"You have left your first love."*

We find the same lack in the church of the present day. There is zeal for the truth, there is continuous and persevering labor, but what the Lord values most is still missing: the tender, fervent love for Himself.

This is a thought of great significance. A church, or even an individual Christian, may be an example in every good work, and yet the tender love for the Lord Jesus in the inner chamber is missing. There is no personal, daily fellowship with Christ, and all the manifold activities with which people satisfy themselves are nothing in the eyes of the Master Himself.

Dear brother or sister in Christ, this book speaks of the fellowship of love that we can have with Christ in the inner chamber. Everything depends on this. Christ came from heaven to love us with the love with which the Father loved Him (John 17:26). He suffered and died to win our hearts for this love. His love can be satisfied with nothing less than a deep, personal love on our part.

Christ considers this of the highest importance. Let us have the same thought. Many ministers, missionaries, and Christian workers confess with shame that, in spite of all their zeal in the Lord's work, their prayer lives are defective because they have left their first love. I pray that you will write this down on a piece of paper and remember it continually: the love of Jesus must be all—in the inner chamber, in all our work, and in our daily lives.

11

THE HOLY SPIRIT

He will glorify Me, for He will take of what is Mine
and declare it to you.
—John 16:14

Our Lord, on the last night that He was with His disciples, promised to send the Holy Spirit as a Comforter. Although His bodily presence was removed, they would realize His presence in them and with them in a wonderful way. The Holy Spirit would so reveal Christ in their hearts, that they would experience His presence with them continually. The Spirit would glorify Christ and would reveal the glorified Christ in heavenly love and power.

How little do Christians understand, believe, and experience this glorious truth! Ministers would fail in their duties if, in a book like this or in their preaching, they encouraged Christians to love the Lord Jesus without at the same time warning them that it is not a duty they can perform in their own strength. No, that is impossible; it is God, the Holy Spirit alone, who will pour out His love in our hearts (Romans 5:5) and will teach us to love Him fervently. Through the Holy Spirit we may experience the love and abiding presence of the Lord Jesus throughout the day.

But let us remember that the Spirit of God must have entire possession of us. He claims our hearts and our entire lives. He will strengthen us with might in the inner man (Ephesians 3:16), so that we may have fellowship with Christ, keep His commandments, and abide in His love.

Once we have grasped this truth, we will begin to feel our deep dependence on the Holy Spirit and will ask the Father to send Him in power into our hearts. The Spirit will teach us to love the Word, to meditate on it, and to keep it. He will reveal the love of Christ to us, so that we may love Him *"fervently with a pure heart"* (1 Peter 1:22). Then we will begin to see that having the love of Christ in the midst of our daily lives and distractions is a glorious possibility and a blessed reality.

12

CHRIST'S LOVE FOR US

Even as the Father hath loved me, I also have loved you:
abide ye in my love.
—John 15:9 RV

In fellowship between friends and relations, everything depends on their love for each other. Of what value is great wealth if love is lacking between husband and wife, or between parents and children? And in our religion, of what value is all knowledge and zeal in God's work, without the knowledge and experience of Christ's love? (See 1 Corinthians 13:1–3.) Oh Christians, the one thing needed in the inner chamber is to know by experience how much Christ loves you, and to learn how you may abide and continue in that love.

Think of what Christ said: *"As the Father hath loved me"*—what a divine, everlasting, wonderful love—*"I also have loved you."* It was the same love with which He had loved the Father and that He always bore in His heart, which He now gave into the hearts of His disciples. He yearns that this everlasting love will rest upon us and work within us, so that we may abide in it day by day. What a blessed life! Christ desires every disciple to live in the power of the very same love of God that He Himself experienced. Reader, do you realize that in your fellowship with Christ in secret or in public, you are surrounded by and kept in this heavenly love? Let your desire reach out for this everlasting love. The Christ with whom you desire fellowship longs unspeakably to fill you with His love.

Read all that God's Word says about the love of Christ. Meditate on the words, and let them sink into your heart. Sooner or later you will begin to realize, "The greatest happiness of my life is that I am loved by the Lord Jesus. I may live in fellowship with Him all day long." Let your heart continually say, "His love for me is unspeakable; He will keep me abiding in His love."

13

OUR LOVE FOR CHRIST

Jesus Christ: whom not having seen ye love; on whom, though now ye see him not, yet believing, ye rejoice greatly with joy unspeakable and full of glory.
—1 Peter 1:8 RV

What a wonderful description of the Christian life! People had never seen Christ, yet they truly loved Him and believed in

Him, so that their hearts were filled with unspeakable joy. Such is the life of a Christian who really loves his Lord.

We have seen that the chief attributes of the Father and the Son are love for each other and love for man. These should be the chief characteristics of the true Christian. The love of God and of Christ is poured out in his heart (Romans 5:5) and becomes a well of living water, flowing forth as love for the Lord Jesus.

This love is not merely a blessed feeling. It is an active principle. It takes pleasure in doing the will of the beloved Lord. It is joy to keep His commandments. The love of Christ for us was shown by His death on the cross; our love must be exhibited in unselfish, selfsacrificing living. Oh, that we understood this: in the Christian life, love for Christ is everything!

Great love will beget great faith—faith in His love for us, faith in the powerful revelations of His love in our hearts, faith that He through His love will work all His good pleasure in us. The wings of faith and love will lift us up to heaven, and we will be filled with *"joy unspeakable."* The joy of the Christian is an indispensable witness to the world of the power of Christ to change hearts and to fill them with heavenly love and gladness.

Oh, you who love the Lord Jesus, take time daily in the inner chamber with Him to drink in a fresh supply of His heavenly love. It will make you strong in faith, and your joy will be full. Love, joy, faith—these will fill your life each day through the grace of the Lord Jesus.

14

LOVE FOR FELLOW CHRISTIANS

A new commandment I give to you, that you love one another; as I have loved you, that you also love one another.
—John 13:34

The Lord Jesus told His disciples that He loved them just as the Father had loved Him. And now, following His example, we must love one another with the same love.

"By this all will know that you are My disciples, if you have love for one another" (v. 35). Christ later prayed, *"That they all may be one, as You, Father, are in Me, and I in You; that they also may be one in Us, that the world may believe that You sent Me"* (John 17:21). If we exhibit the love that was in God toward Christ, and in Christ toward us, the world will be obliged to confess that our Christianity is genuine and from above.

This is what actually happened in Bible times. The Greeks and Romans, Jews and heathen, hated each other. Among all the nations of the world, there was hardly a thought of love for each other. The very idea of selfsacrifice was a strange one. When the unsaved saw that Christians from different nations, under the powerful workings of the Holy Spirit, became one and loved one another, even to the point of selfsacrifice in time of plague or illness, they were amazed and said, "Behold how these people love one another!" (See John 13:35.)

Among professing Christians, there is a certain oneness of belief and feeling of brotherhood, but Christ's heavenly love is often lacking, and we do not bear one another's burdens or love others as heartily as we should. Pray that you will love your fellow believers with the same love with which Christ loves you. If we abide in Christ's love and let that love fill our hearts, supernatural power will be given to us to love all God's children. As the bond of love between the Father and the Son, and between Christ and His followers, is close, so must the bond of love be between all God's children.

15

LOVE FOR SOULS

He who turns a sinner from the error of his way
will save a soul from death.
—James 5:20

What a wonderful thought, that I may save a soul from everlasting death! How can this be? I must convert him from the error of his ways. This is the calling not only of the minister, but also of every Christian: to work for the salvation of sinners.

When Christ and His love takes possession of our hearts, He gives us this love so that we might bring others to Him. In this way, Christ's kingdom is extended. Everyone who has the love of Christ in his heart is commissioned to tell others. This was the case in the early church. After the Day of Pentecost, people went out and told of the love of Christ, which they had themselves experienced. Heathen writers have told us that the rapid spread of Christianity in the first century was due to the fact that each convert, being filled with the love of Christ, tried to deliver the Good News to others.

What a change has come over the church! Many Christians never try to win others to Christ. Their love is so weak and faint that they have no desire to help others. May the time soon come when Christians will feel constrained to tell of the love of Christ. In a particular revival in Korea, the converts were filled with such a burning love for Christ that they felt bound to tell others of His love. It was even taken as a test of membership that each one should have brought another to the Lord before being admitted to the church.

Reader, examine your heart. Pray that, in fellowship with Christ, you will not only think of your own soul, but having received the gift of God's love, will also pass it on to others. You will then know true happiness, the joy of bringing souls to Christ.

Let us pray earnestly to be so filled with God's love that we may wholeheartedly surrender ourselves to win others for Him.

16

THE SPIRIT OF LOVE

*The love of God has been poured out in our hearts by the
Holy Spirit who was given to us.*
—Romans 5:5

The fruit of the Spirit is love.
—Galatians 5:22

When we consider Christ's love for us, our love for Christ, and our love for fellow Christians or for souls around us, the thought sometimes arises: "The demand is too great; it is unattainable; it is impossible for a Christian to live this life of love and to show it to others in the church and to needy souls." And because we deem it impossible, and because of our unbelief and lack of faith in God's promises, we make little progress in this spirit of love.

We need to remind ourselves continually that it is not in our own strength, or even by serious thought, that we can obtain the love of Christ. We must realize the truth that the love of God is *poured out in our hearts* and will be poured out daily by the Spirit of God. Only as we are wholly surrendered to the leading of the Spirit will we be able to live according to God's will. When the inner life of love is renewed from day to day, we will feel compelled to work for souls.

Here is a prayer that you can offer: "*I bow my knees to the Father…that He would grant you…to be strengthened with might through His Spirit in the inner man, that Christ may dwell in your hearts through faith; that you, being rooted and grounded in love, may…know the love of Christ which passes knowledge*" (Ephesians 3:14, 16–19). You may be "*rooted and grounded*" in this love and may know the love "*which passes knowledge*," but only on one condition: you must be strengthened by the Spirit "*in the inner man,*" so that Christ may dwell in your heart. Then you will indeed be "*rooted and grounded in love.*"

Christian, take this message from God's Word, and let it influence your life. Unless you wait upon God daily, on your knees, for His Spirit to be revealed in your heart, you cannot live in this love. A life of prayer will cause you to experience the blessed reality of the love of Christ, the love of fellow believers, and love for souls.

Put your confidence each day in secret in the Holy Spirit—the Spirit of love that God will give to those who ask in faith.

17

PERSEVERING PRAYER

Men always ought to pray and not lose heart.
—Luke 18:1

Continuing steadfastly in prayer.
—Romans 12:12

Pray without ceasing.
—1 Thessalonians 5:17

One of the greatest drawbacks to the life of prayer is that the answer does not come as speedily as we expect. We are discouraged by the thought, "Perhaps I do not pray correctly," and so we do not persevere in prayer. This was a lesson that our Lord taught often and urgently. If we look further into the matter, we can see that there may be a reason for the delay, and the waiting may bring a blessing to our souls. Remember Daniel, who waited twenty-one days for the answer to his prayer. (See Daniel 10:1–15.)

When we pray, our desire must grow deeper and stronger, and we must ask with the whole heart. God puts us into the school of persevering prayer so that our weak faith may be strengthened. Believe that there is a great blessing in the delayed answer to prayer.

Above all, God wants to draw us into closer fellowship with Himself. When our prayers are not answered, we learn to realize that the fellowship, nearness, and love of God are more to us than the answers to our petitions, and we continue in prayer. What a blessing Jacob received through the delay of the answer to his prayer! He saw God face-to-face, and as a prince he had power with God and prevailed. (See Genesis 32:28.)

Christians, listen to this warning. Do not be impatient or discouraged if the answer does not come. Rather, continue in prayer. *"Pray without ceasing."* You will find it an unspeakable blessing to do so. You may ask whether your prayer agrees with God's will and His Word. You may inquire if it is in the right spirit and in the name of Christ. Keep on praying; you will learn that the delay in the answer to prayer is one of the most precious means of grace that God can bestow on you. You will also learn that those who have persevered in pleading God's promises are those who have had the greatest power with God in prayer.

18

THE PRAYER MEETING

These all continued with one accord in
prayer and supplication.
—Acts 1:14

And they were all filled with the Holy Spirit.
—Acts 2:4

The value of a genuine prayer meeting is enormous. There God's children meet together, not as in church, to listen to one speaker, but to lift up their hearts unitedly to God. By this means, Christians are drawn closer to each other. Those who are weak are strengthened and encouraged by the testimony of the older and more experienced members, and even young Christians have the opportunity to tell of the joy of the Lord.

The prayer meeting may become a great power for good in a congregation and a spiritual help to both minister and members. By means of intercession, God's blessing is poured out at home and abroad.

But there are also dangers to be considered. Many attend and are edified but never learn to pray themselves. Others go for the sake of social and religious fervor and have a "*form of godliness*" (2 Timothy 3:5) but do not know the hidden life of prayer. Unless there is much and earnest prayer in the inner chamber, attendance at a prayer meeting may be a mere form.

It is well to ask, "What constitutes a living prayer meeting?" There should be hearty love and fellowship between the members.

The leaders should realize how great the influence of such a meeting may be, with its roots nourished by the life of prayer in the inner chamber. Prayer should include God's people and His church all over the world. Above all, as on the Day of Pentecost, there must be waiting on God for the filling of the Holy Spirit.

Dear reader, I aim to help you in your spiritual life. But remember, you do not live for yourself alone; you are part of the body of Christ. You must include all Christians in your intercession. As the roots of the tree hidden deep in the earth are one with the branches that spread out to the sky, so the hidden prayer life is inseparably bound with united prayer.

19

INTERCESSION

Praying always…in the Spirit…with all perseverance and supplication for all the saints.
—Ephesians 6:18

What an unspeakable blessing there is in intercession! That one should pray down heavenly gifts on himself is a wonder of grace, but that he should bring down blessings on others is indeed an inconceivable honor. But God makes the pouring out of blessing on others dependent on our prayers. Indeed, He makes us His remembrancers and fellow workers. He has taken us into partnership in His work; if we fail in doing our part, others will suffer, and His work will suffer unspeakable loss.

God has appointed intercession as one of the means by which souls are saved, and by which saints and ministers of the Gospel are built up in the faith. Even the ends of the earth will receive life and blessing through our prayers. Should we not expect God's children to strive joyfully and with all their powers, by means of intercession, to bring down blessing on the world?

Christian, begin to use intercession as a means of grace for yourself and for others. Pray for your neighbors. Pray for souls with the definite desire that they may be won for Christ. Pray for your minister, for all ministers and missionaries. Pray for your country and its people. Pray for all men. If you surrender yourself to the guidance of the Holy Spirit and live a life wholly for God, you will realize that the time spent in prayer is an offering well pleasing to God, bringing blessing to yourself and power into the lives of those for whom you pray.

Yes, pray *"always with all prayer and supplication in the Spirit, being watchful to this end with all perseverance and supplication for all the saints"* (v. 18). In so doing, you will learn the lesson that intercession is the chief means of winning souls and of bringing glory to God.

20

PRAYER AND FASTING

So Jesus said to them, "Because of your unbelief....However, this kind does not go out except by prayer and fasting."
—Matthew 17:20–21

Our Lord here taught us that a life of faith requires both prayer and fasting. That is, prayer grasps the power of heaven, and fasting loosens the hold on earthly pleasure.

Jesus Himself fasted to get strength to resist the Devil. He taught His disciples that fasting should be in secret and that the heavenly Father would reward openly (Matthew 6:6). Abstinence from food, or moderation in taking it, helps to strengthen the soul for communion with God.

Let us learn this great lesson that abstinence, moderation, and selfdenial in temporal things are a help to the spiritual life. After eating a hearty meal, one does not feel much desire to pray. To willingly sacrifice our own pleasure or bodily enjoyment, and to subdue the lust of the flesh and the lust of the eyes, will help to set our minds more fully on heavenly things. The very exertion needed in overcoming the desires of the flesh will give us strength to take hold of God in prayer.

The great lesson is this: our dullness in prayer comes from our fleshly desires for comfort and ease. *"Those who are Christ's have crucified the flesh with its passions and desires"* (Galatians 5:24). Prayer is not easy work. It may easily become a mere form. For the real practice of prayer, to really take hold of God and have communion with Him, it is necessary that all that can please the flesh is sacrificed and given over to death.

Beloved Christian, it is worth any trouble to deny ourselves daily, in order to meet the holy God and receive heavenly blessings from Him.

21

THE SPIRIT OF PRAYER

The Spirit…makes intercession for the saints.
—Romans 8:27

Prayer is not our work, but God's work, which He works within us by His almighty power. As we consider this statement, our attitude should be one of silent expectation that as we pray, the Holy Spirit will help our weaknesses and will pray within us with *"groanings which cannot be uttered"* (v. 26).

What a thought! When I feel how defective my prayers are, when I have no strength of my own, I may bow in silence before God in the confidence that His Holy Spirit will teach me to pray. The Spirit is the Spirit of prayer. It is not my work, but God's work in me. My desire to pray is a sign that God will hear me.

When God moves to grant our requests, He first works the desire in our hearts, and the Spirit will perfect the work, even in our weakness. We see this in the story of Jacob. The same One who wrestled with him and seemed to withhold the blessing was in reality strengthening him to continue and to prevail in prayer. (See Genesis 32:24–30.) What a wondrous thought! Prayer is the work of the triune God: the Father, who wakens the desire and will give all we need; the Son, who through His intercession teaches us to pray in His name; and the Holy Spirit, who in secret will strengthen our feeble desires.

I have already told you about the Spirit of truth, who will glorify Christ in us, and of the Spirit of love, who will pour out this love in our hearts. Now we have the Spirit of prayer, through whom our lives may be ones of continual prayer. Thank God. The Spirit has been given from heaven to dwell in our hearts and to teach us to pray.

Christian, listen to the leading of the Spirit. Obey His voice in all things. He will make you a man or woman of prayer. You will then realize the glory of your calling as an intercessor, asking great things of God for those around you, for the church, and for the whole unsaved world.

22

WHOLLY FOR CHRIST

*One died for all...that they which live should
no longer live unto themselves, but unto him who for their
sakes died and rose again.*
—2 Corinthians 5:14–15 RV

Here we have a threefold life described. First is the life of the Christian who lives according to his old nature: he lives for himself alone. The second is the life of a true Christian: he lives wholly for Christ. Third is the life of Christ in heaven: He lives wholly for us.

Many Christians need to be convinced of the foolishness of living only for themselves. At conversion, they tend to think more of their own salvation and less of the glory of God and the claim that Christ, who has redeemed us with His precious blood, has upon them. Many Christians live for themselves, content with doing a little for the Master. The believer who realizes his high calling and the privilege and blessedness of consecrating His life entirely to God's service will find true happiness.

The great hindrance to such a life is unbelief, which says that complete submission to God is impossible. But when the truth takes hold of us—"Christ in heaven lives wholly for me; He will impart His life to me and will enable me to live wholly for Him"—then we will be able to say joyfully, "Dear Lord Jesus, from this moment let my prayer each day be, 'Wholly for Christ, wholly for Christ.'"

Dear brother or sister, let nothing less than this be your earnest desire, your prayer, and your firm expectation. Say, "Christ has not only died for me, but He also lives in heaven to keep and sanctify me, His purchased possession." Ponder this wonderful thought: that Christ will keep you as a member of His body, to work and live for Him. Pray for grace to live wholly for God in seeking souls and in serving His people. Take time from day to day to be so united to Christ in the inner man that you can say with all your heart, "I live wholly for Him, who gave Himself wholly for me and who now lives in heaven wholly for me."

23

THE CROSS OF CHRIST

I have been crucified with Christ.
—Galatians 2:20

The cross of Christ is His greatest glory. Because He humbled Himself to the death of the cross, God has highly exalted Him. (See Philippians 2:8–9.) The cross was the power that conquered Satan and sin.

The Christian shares with Christ in the cross. The crucified Christ lives in him through the Holy Spirit, and the spirit of the cross inspires him. He lives as one who has died with Christ. As he realizes the power of Christ's crucifixion, he lives as one who has died to the world and to sin, and the power becomes a reality in his life. It is as the Crucified One that Christ lives in him.

Our Lord said to His disciples, *"Take up [your] cross, and follow Me"* (Matthew 16:24). Did they understand this? They had seen men carrying a cross, and they knew it meant a painful death. All His life, Christ bore His cross—the death sentence that He would die for the world. Similarly, each Christian must bear his cross, acknowledge that he is worthy of death, and believe that he is crucified with Christ and that the Crucified One lives in him. *"Our old man was crucified with Him"* (Romans 6:6). *"Those who are Christ's have crucified the flesh with its passions and desires"* (Galatians 5:24). When we have accepted this life of the cross, we will be able to say with Paul, *"But God forbid that I should boast except in the cross of our Lord Jesus Christ"* (Galatians 6:14).

This is a deep spiritual truth. Think and pray over it, and the Holy Spirit will teach you. Let the disposition of Christ on the cross, His humility, His sacrifice of all worldly honor, His spirit of selfdenial, take possession of you. The power of His death will work in you, you will become like Him in His death, and you will *"know Him and the power of His resurrection"* (Philippians 3:10). Take time, dear reader, so that Christ through His Spirit may reveal Himself as the Crucified One.

24

THE WORLD

Do not love the world or the things in the world.
If anyone loves the world, the love of the Father is not in him.
—1 John 2:15

John taught us clearly what he meant by *"the world."* He wrote, *"All that is in the world; the lust of the flesh, the lust of the eyes, and the pride of life; is not of the Father but is of the world"* (v. 16).

The world is the disposition or power under which man has fallen through sin. And the god of this world, in order to deceive man, conceals himself under the form of what God has created. The world, with its pleasures, surrounds the Christian each day with temptations.

This was the case with Eve in the Garden of Eden. In Genesis 3:6, we find the three characteristics that John mentioned: first, the lust of the flesh: *"The woman saw that the tree was good for food"*; second, the lust of the eyes: *"It was pleasant to the eyes"*; and third, the pride of life: *"A tree desirable to make one wise."* The world still comes to us offering desirable food and much to please the fleshly appetites. It offers much that the eye desires, including riches, beauty, and luxury. And it offers the pride of life, which is shown when a man imagines he knows and understands everything, and prides himself on it.

Are our lives in the world not full of danger, with the allurements of the flesh, so much to occupy our eyes and our hearts, and so much worldly wisdom and knowledge?

John told us, "Do not love the world, for then the love of the Father is not in you." Our Lord calls us, as He called His disciples, to leave all and follow Him.

Christian, you live in a dangerous world. Cling to the Lord Jesus. As He teaches you to shun the world and its attractions, your love will go out to Him in loyal-hearted service. But remember, there must be daily fellowship with Jesus. His love alone can expel the love of the world. Take time to be alone with your Lord.

25

PUT ON CHRIST

For as many of you as were baptized into Christ
have put on Christ.
—Galatians 3:27

Put on the Lord Jesus Christ, and make
no provision for the flesh, to fulfill its lusts.
—Romans 13:14

The word that is translated *"put on"* is the same that is used in regard to putting on clothes. We have *"put on the new man"* (Ephesians 4:24), and the new nature is like a garment that is worn so that all can see who we are. Paul said that the Christian, when he has confessed Christ at baptism, has *"put on Christ."* Just as a man may be recognized by the garment he wears, so the Christian is known by the fact that he has put on Christ and exhibits Him in his whole life and character.

"Put on the Lord Jesus," not just at conversion, but also on a daily basis. As I put on my clothes each day and am seen in them, so the Christian must daily put on the Lord Jesus, so that he no longer lives to fulfill the lusts of the flesh, but shows forth the image of his Lord and the new man formed in His likeness.

Put on Christ! This work must be done each day in the inner chamber. I must put on the Lord, the heavenly Jesus. But I need time to put on Christ. Just as my garments cover me and protect me from the wind and the sun, even so Christ Jesus will be my beauty, my defense, and my joy. As I commune with Him in prayer, He imparts Himself to me and strengthens me to walk as one who is in Him and is bound to Him forever.

Reader, take time to meditate on this wonderful truth. Just as your clothing is a necessity as you go out into the world, let it be equally indispensable for you to put on Jesus Christ, to abide in Him, and to walk with Him all day long.

This cannot be done hastily and superficially. It takes time, quiet time in living fellowship with Jesus, to realize that you have put Him on. Take the time and the trouble. Your reward will be great.

26

THE STRENGTH OF THE CHRISTIAN

Finally, my brethren, be strong in the Lord
and in the power of His might.
—Ephesians 6:10

As the apostle reached the end of his epistle, he began the last section of it with the words, *"Finally, my brethren, be strong in the Lord."*

The Christian needs strength. This we all know. We also know the truth that the Christian has no strength of his own. Where may strength be obtained? Notice the answer: *"Be strong in the Lord and in the power of His might."*

Paul had spoken of this power in the earlier part of his epistle. He had prayed, "God, give them the Spirit, that they might know *'the exceeding greatness of His power…according to the working of His mighty power which He worked in Christ when He raised Him from the dead'* (Ephesians 1:19–20)." This is the literal truth: *"the exceeding greatness of His power,"* which raised Christ from the dead, works in every believer—in me and in you. We hardly believe it, and we experience it even less. This is why Paul prayed, and we must pray with him, that God through His Spirit would teach us to believe in His almighty power. Pray with all your heart: "Father, grant me the Spirit of wisdom, so that I may experience this power in my life."

In Ephesians 3, Paul asked God to grant the Ephesians, *"according to the riches of His glory, to be strengthened with might through His Spirit in the inner man, that Christ may dwell in* [their] *hearts"* (vv. 16–17). And then he added, *"Now to Him who is able to do exceedingly abundantly above all that we ask or think, according to the power that works in us, to Him be glory"* (vv. 20–21).

Read over these two passages again, and pray for God's Spirit to enlighten your eyes. Believe in the divine power working within you. Pray that the Holy Spirit will reveal it to you, and take hold of the promise that God will manifest His power in your heart, supplying all your needs.

Have you not begun to realize that much time in communion with the Father and the Son is necessary if you want to experience the power of God within you?

27

THE WHOLE HEART

With my whole heart I have sought You.
—Psalm 119:10

Notice how often the psalmist spoke about the whole heart in Psalm 119: "*Those…who seek Him with the whole heart*" (v. 2); "*I shall observe* [Your law] *with my whole heart*" (v. 34); "*I will keep Your precepts with my whole heart*" (v. 69); "*I cry out with my whole heart*" (v. 145). In seeking God, in observing His law, in crying for His help—each time it is with the whole heart.

When we want to make anything a success in worldly affairs, we put our whole heart into it. Is this not much more necessary in the service of the holy God? Is He not worthy? Does His great holiness, and the natural aversion of our hearts from God, not demand it? The whole heart is needed in the service of God when we worship Him in secret.

And yet how little most Christians think of this! They do not remember how necessary it is in prayer, in reading God's Word, in striving to do His will, to say continually, "*With my whole heart I have sought You.*" Yes, when we pray, and when we try to understand God's Word and obey His commands, let us say, "I desire to seek God, to serve Him, and to please Him with my whole heart."

"*With my whole heart I have sought You.*" Dear reader, take these words into your heart. Think over them. Pray over them. Speak them out before God until you feel, "I really mean what I say, and I have the assurance that God will hear my prayer." Say them each morning as you approach God in prayer: "I seek You with my whole heart." You will soon feel the need of waiting in holy stillness upon God, so that He may take possession of your whole heart, and you will learn to love Him with your whole heart and with all your strength.

28

IN CHRIST

But of [God] you are in Christ Jesus.
—1 Corinthians 1:30

The expression "*in Christ*" is often used in the Epistles. The Christian cannot read God's Word correctly, nor experience its full power in his life, until he prayerfully and believingly accepts this truth: I am in Christ Jesus.

The Lord Jesus, on the last night with His disciples, used this expression more than once. He said that when the Spirit had been poured out, "*at that day you will know that I am in My Father, and you in Me*" (John 14:20). And then follows, "*Abide in Me....He who abides in Me, and I in him, bears much fruit*" (John 15:4–5); "*If you abide in Me...you will ask what you desire, and it shall be done for you*" (v. 7). But the Christian cannot take hold of these promises unless he first prayerfully accepts the words, "*in Christ.*"

Paul expressed the same thought in Romans: "*We [are] buried with Him*" (Romans 6:4); we are "*dead indeed to sin, but alive to God in Christ Jesus our Lord*" (v. 11); "*There is therefore now no condemnation to those who are in Christ Jesus*" (Romans 8:1). In Ephesians, Paul wrote that God "*has blessed us with every spiritual blessing…in Christ*" (Ephesians 1:3); He "*chose us in Him*" (v. 4); and "*He has made us accepted in the Beloved. In Him we have redemption*" (vv. 6–7). And in Colossians we find: "*In Him dwells all the fullness*" (Colossians 2:9); we are "*perfect in Christ Jesus*" (Colossians 1:28); "*walk in Him*" (Colossians 2:6); and "*you are complete in Him*" (v. 10). '

Let your faith take hold of these words: it is God who establishes us in Christ (2 Corinthians 1:21). "*Of [God] you are in Christ Jesus.*" The Holy Spirit will make it your experience. Pray earnestly, and follow the leading of the Spirit. The word will take root in your heart, and you will realize something of its heavenly power. But remember that abiding in Christ is a matter of the heart. It must be cultivated in a spirit of love. Only as you take time from day to day in fellowship with Christ will the abiding in Christ become a blessed reality, and the inner man will be renewed from day to day.

29

CHRIST IN ME

Do you not know…that Jesus Christ is in you?
—2 Corinthians 13:5

The apostle Paul wanted each Christian to live in the full assurance of "Christ is in me." What a difference it would make in our lives if we could take time every morning to be filled with the thought, "Christ is in me"! As surely as I am in Christ, Christ is also in me.

On His last night on earth, Christ clearly told His disciples that the Spirit would teach them: *"At that day you will know that I am in My Father, and you in Me, and I in you"* (John 14:20). Through the power of God, all of us who believe were crucified with Christ and raised again with Him. As a result, Christ is in us. But this knowledge does not come easily. Through faith in God's Word, we Christians accept it, and the Holy Spirit will lead us into all truth (John 16:13). Take time this very day to realize and take hold of this blessing in prayer.

Paul clearly expressed this thought in the prayer of Ephesians 3:16–17: *"That* [the Father] *would grant you, according to the riches of His glory"*—notice that it is not the ordinary gift of grace, but a special revelation of the riches of His love and power—*"to be strengthened with might through His Spirit in the inner man, that Christ may dwell in your hearts through faith."* Have you grasped it? Every Christian may really have the experience of being filled with the fullness of God.

Dear Christian, Paul said, *"I bow my knees to the Father"* (v. 14). That is the only way to obtain the blessing. Take time in the inner chamber to realize, "Christ dwells in me. Too little have I experienced this in the past, but I will cry to God and wait upon Him to perfect His work in me. Even in the midst of my daily work, I must look upon my heart as the dwelling place of the Son of God, and say, 'I am crucified with Christ. I live no more; Christ lives in me.' (See Galatians 2:20.) Only in this way will Christ's words, *'Abide in Me, and I in you'* (John 15:4), become my daily experience."

30

CHRIST IS ALL

Christ is all and in all.
—Colossians 3:11

In the eternal counsel of God, in the redemption on the cross, and as King on the throne in heaven and on earth, *"Christ is all."* In the salvation of sinners, in their justification and sanctification, in the upbuilding of Christ's body, and in the care for individuals, even the most sinful, *"Christ is all."* Every day and every hour, the child of God is comforted and strengthened when he accepts, in faith, that *"Christ is all."*

Perhaps you have thought in reading these pages that the full salvation here described is not meant for you. You feel too weak, too unworthy, too untrustworthy. My dear reader, if you will only accept the Lord Jesus in childlike faith, you will have a Leader and a Guide who will supply all your needs (Philippians 4:19). Believe with your whole heart in the words of our Savior—*"Lo, I am with you always"* (Matthew 28:20)—and you will experience His presence each day.

However cold and dull your feelings may be, however sinful you are, meet the Lord Jesus in secret, and He will reveal Himself to you. Tell Him how wretched you are, and then trust Him to help and sustain you. Wait before Him until by faith you can rejoice in Him. Read this book over again, and read it with the thought, *"Christ is all."* You may have failed to remember this at times, but each day as you go into secret prayer, let this thought be with you: *"Christ is all."* Take it as your motto, to teach you to pray, to strengthen your faith, to give you the assurance of His love and access to the Father, to make you strong for the work of the day. *"Christ is all."* Yes, Christ, your Christ, is all you need. This will teach you to abide in His love. It will give you the assurance that He dwells in your heart, and you may know *"the love…which passes knowledge"* (Ephesians 3:19). God be praised to all eternity! Christ, your Christ, is your all in all!

31

INTERCESSION

Pray for one another.
—James 5:16

What a mystery of glory there is in prayer! On the one hand, we see God, in His holiness and love and power, waiting, longing to bless man; on the other, we see sinful man, a worm of the dust, bringing down from God by prayer the very life and love of heaven to dwell in his heart.

But how much greater the glory of intercession! Through it a man comes boldly to God to say what he desires for others, and through it he seeks to bring down on one soul—or even on hundreds and thousands—the power of eternal life with all its blessings.

Intercession! Would you not say that this is the holiest exercise of our boldness as God's children, the highest privilege and enjoyment connected with our communion with God? It is the power of being used by God as instruments for His great work of making men His habitation and showing forth His glory.

Would you not think that the church would consider this one of the chief means of grace, and seek above everything to cultivate in God's children the power of an unceasing prayerfulness on behalf of the perishing world?

Would you not expect that believers, who have to some extent been brought into the secret of intercession, would feel what strength there is in unity, and what assurance there is that God will certainly *"avenge His own elect who cry out day and night to Him"* (Luke 18:7)? When Christians cease from looking for help in external union, and aim at being bound together to the throne of God by an unceasing devotion to Jesus Christ and by an unceasing continuance in supplication for the power of God's Spirit, the church will put on her beautiful garments and her strength (Isaiah 52:1), and will overcome the world.

> Our gracious Father, hear our prayer, and teach Your church and each of us what is the glory, the blessing, and the allprevailing power of intercession. Give us, we pray, the vision of what intercession means to You, how it is essential for carrying out Your blessed purpose and in the bringing down of the Spirit in power. Show us what it means to us as the exercise of our royal priesthood, and what it will mean to Your church and to perishing men. Amen.

32

THE OPENING OF THE EYES

And Elisha prayed, and said,
*"L*ORD*, I pray, open his eyes that he may see....*
L*ORD*, *open the eyes of these men, that they may see."*
—2 Kings 6:17, 20

How wonderfully the prayer of Elisha for his servant was answered! The young man saw the mountain full of chariots of fire and horsemen surrounding Elisha. The heavenly host had been sent by God to protect the Lord's servant.

Then Elisha prayed a second time. The Syrian army had been stricken with blindness and were led into Samaria. There Elisha prayed for the opening of their eyes, and they found themselves hopeless prisoners in the hand of the enemy.

We ought to use these prayers in the spiritual sphere. First of all, we ought to ask that our eyes may see the wonderful provision that God has made for His church, in the baptism with the Holy Spirit and with fire. (See Matthew 3:11.) All the powers of the heavenly world are at our disposal in the service of the heavenly kingdom. How little the children of God live in the faith of that heavenly vision—the power of the Holy Spirit on them, with them, and in them, for their own spiritual life and as their strength to joyfully witness for their Lord and His work!

But we will find that we need that second prayer, too, so that God may open the eyes of those of His children who do not yet see the power that the world and sin have upon His people. They are still unaware of the feebleness that marks the church, making it powerless to do the work of winning souls for Christ and building up believers for a life of holiness and fruitfulness. Let us pray especially that God may open all eyes to see what the great and fundamental need of the church is—to bring down His blessing in intercession, so that the power of the Spirit may be known unceasingly in its divine effectiveness and blessing.

Our Father, who is in heaven, You who are so unspeakably willing to give us the Holy Spirit in power, hear our humble prayer. Open our eyes, we pray, so that we may realize fully the low estate of Your church, and that we may know as fully what treasures of grace and power You are willing to bestow in answer to the fervent prayer of a united church. Amen.

33

MAN'S PLACE IN GOD'S PLAN

The heaven, even the heavens, are the Lord's;
but the earth He has given to the children of men.
—Psalm 115:16

God created heaven as a dwelling for Himself—perfect, glorious, and most holy. The earth He gave to man as his dwelling—everything very good, but only as a beginning, with the need of being kept and cultivated. Man was to continue and perfect the work God had done. Think of the iron and the coal hidden away in the earth, of the steam hidden away in the water. It was left to man to discover and use all this, as we see in the network of railways that span the world, and the steamers that cover the ocean. God had created everything to be thus used. But He made the discovery and the use of such things dependent on the wisdom and diligence of man. What the earth is today, with its cities and its cornfields, it owes to man. The work God had begun and prepared was to be carried out by man in fulfillment of God's purpose. And so nature teaches us the wonderful partnership to which God calls man for the carrying out of the work of creation to its destined end.

This principle is equally strong in the kingdom of grace. In His great plan of redemption, God has revealed the power of the heavenly life and the spiritual blessings of which heaven is full. But He has entrusted to His people the work of making these blessings known and of making men partakers of them.

What diligence the children of this world show in seeking the treasures that God has hidden in the earth for their use! Will the children of God not be equally faithful in seeking the treasures hidden in heaven, to bring them down in blessings on the world? It is by the unceasing intercession of God's people that His kingdom will come and His will be done on earth as it is in heaven (Luke 11:2).

Ever blessed Lord, how wonderful is the place You have given man, in trusting him to continue the work You have begun. Open our hearts for the great thought that, through the preaching of the Gospel and the work of intercession, Your people are to work out Your purpose. Lord, open our eyes, for Jesus's sake. Amen.

34

INTERCESSION IN THE PLAN OF REDEMPTION

O You who hear prayer, to You all flesh will come.
—Psalm 65:2

When God gave the world into the power of man, who was made in His own image and who was to rule over it as a representative under Him, it was His plan that Adam should do nothing without God, and God Himself would do all His work in the world through Adam. Adam was to be the owner, master, and ruler of the earth. When sin entered the world, Adam's power was proved to be a terrible reality, for through him the earth, with the whole race of man, was brought under the curse of sin.

When God established the plan of redemption, His objective was to restore man to the place from which he had fallen. God chose servants who, through the power of intercession, could ask what they desired, and it would be given to them (John 15:7). When Christ became man, it was so that, as man, both on earth and in heaven, He might intercede for man. And before He left the world, He imparted this right of intercession to His disciples, in the sevenfold promise of the Farewell Discourse (John 15–17), that whatever they would ask, He would do for them. God's intense longing to bless seems in some sense to be graciously limited by His dependence on the intercession that rises from the earth. He seeks to rouse the spirit of intercession so that He may be able to bestow His blessings on mankind. God regards intercession as the highest expression of His people's readiness to receive and to yield themselves wholly to the working of His almighty power.

Christians need to realize this as their true nobility and their only power with God—the right to claim and expect that God will hear prayer. Only as God's children begin to see what intercession means in regard to God's kingdom will they realize how solemn their responsibility is.

Each individual believer will be led to see that God waits for him to take his part. He will feel that the highest, the most blessed, the mightiest of all human positions for the fulfillment of the petition, "as in heaven, so on earth," is the intercession that rises day and night, pleading with God for the power of heaven to be sent down into the hearts of men. Oh, that God might burn into our hearts this one thought: intercession in its omnipotent power is according to His will and is most certainly effective!

35

GOD SEEKS INTERCESSORS

He saw that there was no man,
and wondered that there was no intercessor.
—Isaiah 59:16

In Old Testament times, God had among His people intercessors to whose voices He had listened and given deliverance. In Isaiah 59, we read of a time of trouble when God sought for an intercessor but found none. And He wondered! Think of what that means—the amazement of God that there was no one who loved the people enough or who had enough faith in His power to deliver, that he would intercede on their behalf. If there had been an intercessor, God would have given deliverance; without an intercessor, His judgments came down. (See Ezekiel 22:30–31.)

Of what infinite importance is the place the intercessor holds in the kingdom of God! Is it not indeed a matter of wonder that God should give men such power, and yet there are so few who know what it is to take hold of His strength and to pray down His blessings on the world?

Let us try to realize this position. When God had in His Son worked out the new creation and Christ had taken His place on the throne, the work of the extension of His kingdom was given into the hands of men. All that Christ was to do in heaven was to be in fellowship with His people on earth. In His divine condescension, God has willed that the working of His Spirit will follow the prayers of His people. He waits for their intercession that shows the preparation of their hearts—where and how much of His Spirit they are ready to receive.

God rules the world and His church through the prayers of His people. God calls for intercessors: in His grace He has made His work dependent on them; He waits for them.

Our Father, open our eyes to see that You invite Your children to have a part in the extension of Your kingdom by their faithfulness in prayer and intercession. Give us such an insight into the glory of this holy calling, so that with our whole hearts we may yield ourselves to its blessed service. Amen.

36

CHRIST AS INTERCESSOR

He is also able to save to the uttermost those who
come to God through Him,
since He always lives to make intercession for them.
—Hebrews 7:25

When God had said in Isaiah that He wondered that there was no intercessor, there followed these words: *"Therefore His own arm brought salvation for Him….The Redeemer will come to Zion"* (Isaiah 59:16, 20). God Himself would provide the true Intercessor, in Christ His Son, of whom it had already been said, *"He bore the sin of many, and made intercession for the transgressors"* (Isaiah 53:12).

In His life on earth, Christ began His work as Intercessor. Think of His highpriestly prayer on behalf of His disciples and all who would through them believe in His name. Think of His words to Peter: *"I have prayed for you, that your faith should not fail"* (Luke 22:32)—a proof of how intensely personal His intercession is. And on the cross He spoke as Intercessor: *"Father, forgive them"* (Luke 23:34).

Now that He is seated at God's right hand, He continues, as our great High Priest, the work of intercession without ceasing. But He does so HHHHwith this difference: He gives His people power to take part in it. Seven times in His farewell discourse He repeated the assurance that what they asked He would do.

The power of heaven was to be at their disposal. The grace and power of God waited for man's asking. Through the leading of the Holy Spirit, they would know what the will of God was. They would learn in faith to pray in His name. He would present their petition to the Father, and through His and their united intercession, the church would be clothed with the power of the Spirit.

Blessed Redeemer, what wonderful grace it is that You call us to share in Your intercession! Arouse in Your redeemed people an awareness of the glory of this calling, and of all the rich blessings that Your church in its powerlessness can, through its intercession in Your name, bring down upon this earth. May Your Holy Spirit work in Your people a deep conviction of the sin of prayerlessness, of the sloth and unbelief and selfishness that are the cause of it, and of Your loving desire to pour out the Spirit of prayer in answer to their petitions, for Your name's sake. Amen.

37

THE SCHOOL OF INTERCESSION

Who, in the days of His flesh, when He had offered up
prayers and supplications, with vehement cries and tears…
was heard because of His godly fear.
—Hebrews 5:7

Christ, as the Head of the church, is Intercessor in heaven; we, as the members of His body, are partners with Him on earth. Let no one imagine that it cost Christ nothing to become an intercessor.

He is our example because of the enormous price He paid. What do we read about Him? *"When You make His soul an offering for sin, He shall see His seed….He shall see the labor of His soul….I will divide Him a portion with the great…because He poured out His soul unto death"* (Isaiah 53:10–12). Notice the repeated expression in regard to the pouring out of His soul.

The pouring out of the soul is the divine meaning of intercession. Nothing less than this was needed if His sacrifice and prayer were to have power with God. This giving over of Himself to live and die so that He might save the perishing was a revelation of the spirit that has power to prevail with God.

If we as helpers and fellow laborers with the Lord Jesus are to share His power of intercession, we will need to have the travail of soul that He had, the same giving up of our life and its pleasures for the one supreme work of interceding for our fellowmen. Intercession must not be a passing interest; it must become an ever growing object of intense desire, for which we long and live above everything else. It is the life of consecration and selfsacrifice that will indeed give power for intercession.

The longer we study this blessed truth and think of what it means to exercise this power for the glory of God and the salvation of men, the deeper our conviction will become that it is worth giving up everything to take part with Christ in His work of intercession.

Blessed Lord Jesus, teach us how to unite with You in calling upon God for the souls You have bought. Let Your love fill us and all Your saints, so that we may learn to plead for the power of Your Holy Spirit to be made known. Amen.

38

THE NAME OF JESUS: THE POWER OF INTERCESSION

Until now you have asked nothing in My name.
Ask, and you will receive, that your joy may be full....
In that day you will ask in My name.
—John 16:24, 26

During Christ's life upon earth, the disciples had known little of the power of prayer. In Gethsemane, Peter and the others utterly failed. They had no conception of what it meant to ask in the name of Jesus and to receive. The Lord promised them that in the day that was coming, they would be able to pray with such a power in His name, that they would ask what they desired and it would be given to them.

"Until now...nothing." "In that day you will ask in My name" and *"will receive."* These two conditions are still found in the church. With the great majority of Christians, there is such a lack of knowledge of their oneness with Christ Jesus, and of the Holy Spirit as the Spirit of prayer, that they do not even attempt to claim the wonderful promises Christ gave here. But when God's children know what it means to abide in Christ in vital union with Him and to yield to the Holy Spirit's teaching, they begin to learn that their intercession is effective and that God will give the power of His Spirit in answer to their prayers.

It is faith in the power of Jesus's name and in our right to use it that will give us the courage to follow where God invites us—to the holy office of intercessors. When our Lord Jesus, in His farewell discourse, gave His unlimited prayer promise, He sent the disciples out into the world with this thought: "He who sits upon the throne and lives in my heart has promised that what I ask in His name I will receive. He will do it."

Oh, if Christians only knew what it means to yield themselves wholly and absolutely to Jesus Christ and His service, how their eyes would be opened to see that intense and unceasing prayerfulness is the essential mark of the healthy spiritual life! They would see that the power of allprevailing intercession will indeed be the portion of those who live only in and for their Lord.

> Blessed Savior, give us the grace of the Holy Spirit to live in You, with You, and for You to such a degree that we may boldly look to You for the assurance that our prayers are heard. Amen.

39

PRAYER: THE WORK OF THE SPIRIT

God has sent forth the Spirit of His Son into your hearts,
crying out, "Abba, Father!"
—Galatians 4:6

We know what *"Abba, Father"* meant in the mouth of Christ at Gethsemane. It was the entire surrender of Himself to death, so that the holy will of God's love in the redemption of sinners might be accomplished. In His prayer, He was ready for any sacrifice, even the yielding of His life. In that prayer, the heart of Him whose place is at the right hand of God is revealed to us, with the wonderful power of intercession that He exercises there, and the power to pour down the Holy Spirit.

The Holy Spirit has been bestowed by the Father to breathe the very Spirit of His Son into our hearts. Our Lord desires us to yield ourselves as wholly to God as He did—to pray as He did, that God's will of love would be done on earth at any cost. As God's love is revealed in His desire for the salvation of souls, so also the desire of Jesus was made plain when He gave Himself for them. And He now asks that the same love would fill His people, too, so that they give themselves wholly to the work of intercession and, at any cost, pray down God's love upon the perishing world.

Lest anyone should begin to think that this is beyond his reach, the Holy Spirit of Jesus is actually given into our hearts so that we may pray in His likeness, in His name, and in His power. It is the man who yields himself wholly to the leading of the Holy Spirit who will feel urged, by the compulsion of a divine love, to surrender himself completely to a life of continual intercession, because he knows that it is God who is working in Him.

Now we can understand how Christ could give such unlimited promises of answer to prayer to His disciples: they were first going to be filled with the Holy Spirit. Now we understand how God can give such a high place to intercession in the fulfillment of His purpose of redemption. It is the Holy Spirit who breathes God's own desire into us and enables us to intercede for souls.

"Abba, Father!" Grant that by Your Holy Spirit there may be maintained in us the unceasing intercession of love for the souls for whom Christ died. Give to Your children the vision of the blessedness and power that come to those who yield themselves to this high calling. Amen.

40

CHRIST: OUR EXAMPLE IN INTERCESSION

He shall divide the spoil with the strong, because…He bore the sin of many, and made intercession for the transgressors.
—Isaiah 53:12

Christ *"made intercession for the transgressors."* What did that mean to Him? Think of what it cost Him to pray that prayer effectively. He had to pour out His soul as an offering for sin, and He had to cry at Gethsemane, "Father, Your holy will of love be done."

Think of what moved Him thus to sacrifice Himself to the very uttermost! It was His love for the Father, so that His holiness might be manifested, and His love for souls, so that they might be partakers of His holiness.

Think of the reward He won! As Conqueror of every enemy, He is seated at the right hand of God with the power of unlimited and assured intercession. And He desires to *"see His seed"* (Isaiah 53:10), a generation of those who have the same mind as Himself, whom He can train to share in His great work of intercession.

And what does this mean for us, when we seek to pray for the transgressors? That we, too, yield ourselves wholly to the glory of the holiness and the love of the Father; that we, too, say, "God's will be done, no matter what it may cost"; that we, too, sacrifice ourselves, even to pouring out our souls unto death.

The Lord Jesus has taken us up into a partnership with Himself in carrying out the great work of intercession. He in heaven and we on earth must have one mind, one aim in life: that we, out of love for the Father and for the lost, consecrate our lives to intercession for God's blessing. The burning desire of Father and Son for the salvation of souls must be the burning desire of our hearts, too.

What an honor! What blessedness! And what a power for us to do the work because He lives and because, by His Spirit, He pours forth His love into our hearts (Romans 5:5)!

Everlasting God of love, open our eyes to the vision of the glory of Your Son, who always lives to pray (Hebrews 7:25). Open our eyes to the glory of the grace that enables us to live in His likeness so that we may pray for the transgressors. For Jesus's sake. Amen.

41

GOD'S WILL AND OURS

Your will be done.
—Matthew 26:42

It is the high prerogative of God that everything in heaven and earth is to be done according to His will and as the fulfillment of His desires. When He made man in His image, man's desires were intended to be in perfect accord with the desires of God. This is the high honor of being made in the likeness of God—that we are to feel and wish just as God does. In human flesh, man was to be the embodiment and fulfillment of God's desires.

When God created man with the power of willing and choosing what he should be, He limited Himself in the exercise of His will. And when man had fallen and yielded himself to the will of God's enemy, God in His infinite love set about the great work of winning man back, and of making the desires of God his own. As desire is the great motivating power in God, so it is in man. And just as man had yielded himself to a life of desire after the things of the earth and the flesh, God had to redeem him and educate him into a life of harmony with Himself. His one aim was that man's desires would be in perfect accord with His own.

The great step in this direction was when the Son of the Father came into this world. He reproduced the divine desires in His human nature and in His prayer to yield Himself up to the perfect fulfillment of all that God wished and willed. The Son, as Man, said in agony and blood, *"Your will be done,"* and made the surrender even to being forsaken by God, so that the power that had deceived man might be conquered and deliverance might be procured. It was in the wonderful and complete harmony between the Father and the Son when the Son said, *"Your will* [of love] *be done,"* that the great redemption was accomplished.

In taking hold of that redemption, believers have to say, first of all for themselves and then in lives devoted to intercession for others, "Your will be done in heaven as on earth." (See Matthew 6:10.) As we plead for the church, its ministers, and its missionaries, its strong Christians or its young converts, and for the unsaved, whether nominally Christian or unchurched, we have the privilege of knowing that we are pleading for what God wills, and that through our prayers His will is to be done on earth as in heaven.

42

THE BLESSEDNESS OF A LIFE OF INTERCESSION

*You who make mention of the L*ORD*, do not keep silent,
and give Him no rest till He establishes and till He makes
Jerusalem a praise in the earth.*
—Isaiah 62:6–7

What unspeakable grace to be allowed to deal with God in intercession for the supply of the needs of others!

What a blessing, in close union with Christ, to take part in His great work as Intercessor, and to mingle my prayers with His! What an honor to have power with God in heaven over souls, and to obtain for them what they do not know or think!

What a privilege, as a steward of the grace of God, to bring to Him the state of the church or of individual souls, of the ministers of the Word or His messengers working among the unsaved, and plead on their behalf until He entrusts me with the answer!

What blessedness, in union with other children of God, to strive together in prayer until the victory is gained over difficulties here on earth, or over the powers of darkness in high places!

It is indeed worth living for, to know that God will use me as an intercessor, to receive and dispense here on earth His heavenly blessing and, above all, the power of His Holy Spirit.

This is the life of heaven, the life of the Lord Jesus Himself, in His selfdenying love, taking possession of me and urging me to yield myself wholly to bear the burden of souls before Him, and to plead that they may live.

For too long we have thought of prayer simply as a means for supplying our needs in life and service. May God help us to see the place intercession takes in His divine counsel and in His work for the kingdom. And may our hearts indeed feel that there is no honor or blessedness on earth at all equal to the unspeakable privilege of waiting upon God, and of bringing down from heaven the blessings He delights to give!

Oh my Father, let Your life flow down to this earth, and fill the hearts of Your children! As the Lord Jesus pours out His love in His unceasing intercession in heaven, let it be the same with us also upon earth—a life of overflowing love and never ending intercession. Amen.

43

THE PLACE OF PRAYER

These all continued with one accord in
prayer and supplication.
—Acts 1:14

Christ instructed His disciples to *"wait for the Promise of the Father"* (v. 4). He also said, *"You shall receive power when the Holy Spirit has come upon you; and you shall be witnesses to Me in Jerusalem…and to the end of the earth"* (v. 8).

United and unceasing prayer, the power of the Holy Spirit, living witnesses to the living Christ, from Jerusalem to the end of the earth—such are the marks of the true Gospel, the true ministry, the true church of the New Testament.

A church of united and unceasing prayerfulness, a ministry filled with the Holy Spirit, the members living witnesses to a living Christ, with a message to every creature on earth—such was the church that Christ founded, and such was the church that went out to conquer the world.

When Christ had ascended to heaven, the disciples knew at once what their work was to be: continuing *"with one accord in prayer and supplication."* They were to be bound together, by the love and Spirit of Christ, into one body. This gave them their wonderful power in heaven with God, and upon earth with men.

Their own duty was to wait in united and unceasing prayer for the power of the Holy Spirit, the power to be witnesses for Christ to the end of the earth. A praying church, a Spiritfilled church, a witnessing church, with all the world as its sphere and aim—such is the church of Jesus Christ.

As long as it maintained this character, the church had power to conquer. However, as it came under the influence of the world, how much it lost of its heavenly, supernatural beauty and strength! How unfaithful in prayer, how feeble the workings of the Spirit, how formal its witness to Christ, and how unfaithful to its worldwide mission!

Blessed Lord Jesus, have mercy upon Your church, and give us the Spirit of prayer and supplication as the early church had, so that we may prove what is the power from You that rests upon us and our testimony for You, to win the world to You. Amen.

44

PAUL AS AN INTERCESSOR

I bow my knees to the Father…that He would grant you…
to be strengthened with might through His Spirit.
—Ephesians 3:14, 16

We think of Paul as the great missionary, the great preacher, the great writer, and the great apostle *"in labors more abundant"* (2 Corinthians 11:23). We do not sufficiently think of him as the intercessor who sought and obtained, by his supplication, the power that rested upon all his other activities, and brought down the blessing that rested on the churches that he served.

Look beyond what he wrote to the Ephesians. Think of what he said to the Thessalonians: *"Night and day praying exceedingly that we may see your face and perfect what is lacking in your faith…so that He may establish your hearts blameless in holiness"* (1 Thessalonians 3:10, 13). To the Romans he said, *"Without ceasing I make mention of you always in my prayers"* (Romans 1:9). To the Philippians he wrote, *"Always in every prayer of mine making request for you all with joy"* (Philippians 1:4). And to the Colossians it was, *"[We] do not cease to pray for you….I want you to know what a great conflict I have for you"* (Colossians 1:9; 2:1).

Day and night he cried to God in his intercession for them, that the light and the power of the Holy Spirit might be in them. As earnestly as he believed in the power of his intercession for them, so did he also believe in the blessings that their prayers would bring upon him: *"I beg you…that you strive together with me*

71

in prayers to God for me" (Romans 15:30); "[God] *will still deliver us, you also helping together in prayer for us*" (2 Corinthians 1:10–11); "*Praying…[also] for me…that I may open my mouth boldly*" (Ephesians 6:18–19); "*This will turn out for my deliverance through your prayer*" (Philippians 1:19).

The whole relationship between pastor and people depends on their united, continual prayerfulness. Their whole relationship to each other is a heavenly one, spiritual and divine, and can only be maintained by unceasing prayer. When ministers and people wake up to see that the power and blessing of the Holy Spirit are waiting for their united and unceasing prayer, the church will begin to know something of what Pentecostal apostolic Christianity is.

> Ever blessed Father, we humbly pray that You will restore again graciously to Your church the spirit of supplication and intercession, for Jesus's sake. Amen.

45

INTERCESSION FOR LABORERS

The harvest truly is plentiful, but the laborers are few.
Therefore pray the Lord of the harvest to send
out laborers into His harvest.
—Matthew 9:37–38

The disciples understood very little of what these words meant. Christ gave these words as seeds, to be lodged in their hearts for later use. At Pentecost, as they saw how many of the new converts were ready in the power of the Spirit to testify of Christ, they must have felt that the ten days of continuous united prayer had brought this blessing of laborers in the harvest as the fruit of the Spirit's power.

Christ meant to teach us that, however large the field may be and however few the laborers, prayer is the best, the sure, the only means for supplying the need.

What we need to understand is that prayer must be sent up not only in the time of need, but also in the time of plenty. The whole work is to be carried on in the spirit of prayer, so that the prayer for laborers will be in perfect harmony with the whole of our lives and efforts.

At one time in the China Inland Mission, the number of missionaries had risen to two hundred. But there was still such a deep need for more laborers in some districts that, after much prayer, the attendees at a certain conference felt at liberty to ask God to give them, within a year, one hundred additional laborers and £10,000 (British pounds) to meet the expenses. They agreed to continue in prayer every day throughout the year. At the end of the time, the one hundred suitable men and women had been found, along with £11,000.

To meet the need of the world, its open fields, and its waiting souls, the churches all complain of the lack of laborers and of funds. Does not Christ's voice call us to the united and unceasing prayer that the first disciples had? God is faithful, by the power of His Spirit, to supply every need. Let the church take the posture of united prayer and supplication. God hears prayer.

Blessed Lord Jesus, teach Your church what it means to live and work for You in the spirit of unceasing prayerfulness, so that our faith may rise to the assurance that You will, in a way surpassing all expectations, meet the crying need of a dying world. Amen.

46

INTERCESSION FOR INDIVIDUAL SOULS

You will be gathered one by one, O you children of Israel.
—Isaiah 27:12

In our bodies, every member has its appointed place. The same is true in society and in the church. The work must always aim at the welfare and the highest perfection of the whole, through the cooperation of every individual member.

In the church, the thought is too prevalent that the salvation of men is the work of the minister. But the minister generally only deals with the crowd, seldom reaching the individual. This is the cause of a twofold evil. First, the individual believer does not understand that it is necessary for him to testify to those around him, for the nourishment and strengthening of his own spiritual life and for the ingathering of souls. Second, unconverted souls suffer unspeakable loss because Christ is not personally brought to them by each believer they meet.

Intercession for those around us is far too rare. Its restoration to its right place in the Christian life—how much that would mean to the church and its missions! Oh, when will Christians learn the great truth that what God desires to do needs prayer on earth? As we realize this, we will see that intercession is the chief element in the conversion of souls. All our efforts are futile without the power of the Holy Spirit given in answer to prayer. Only when ministers and people unite in a covenant of prayer and testimony will the church flourish, and every believer will understand the part he has to take.

And what can we do to stir up the spirit of intercession? There is a twofold answer. Every Christian, as he begins to get insight into the need and the power of intercession, must begin to intercede on behalf of single individuals. Pray for your children, for your relatives and friends, for all with whom God brings you into contact. If you find that you do not have the power to intercede, let this discovery humble you and drive you to the mercy seat. God wants every redeemed child of His to intercede for the perishing. Prayer is the vital breath of the normal Christian life, the proof that it is born from above.

Then pray intensely and persistently that God may give the power of His Holy Spirit to you and His children around you, so that the power of intercession may have the place that God will honor.

47

INTERCESSION FOR MINISTERS

Praying always with all prayer and supplication in the Spirit…for all saints—and for me.
—Ephesians 6:18–19

Praying also for us.
—Colossians 4:3

Finally, brethren, pray for us.
—2 Thessalonians 3:1

These expressions of Paul suggest the strength of his conviction that the Christians had power with God and that their prayers would bring new strength to him in his work. Paul had such a sense of the actual unity of the body of Christ, of the interdependence of each member—even the most honorable—on the life that flowed through the whole body, that he sought to rouse Christians, for their own sakes and for his sake and for the sake of the kingdom of God, with this call: *"Continue earnestly in prayer, being vigilant in it with thanksgiving; meanwhile praying also for us"* (Colossians 4:2–3).

The church depends on the ministry to an extent that we very little realize. The place of the minister is so high—he is the steward of the mysteries of God, the ambassador for God to beseech men in Christ's name to be reconciled to Him—that any unfaithfulness or inefficiency in him must bring a terrible blight on the church that he serves. If Paul, after having preached for twenty years in the power of God, still needed the prayers of the church, how much more does the ministry in our day need them?

The minister needs the prayers of his people. He has a right to them. He is dependent on them. It is his task to train Christians for their work of intercession on behalf of the church and the world. He must begin by training them to pray for himself. He may even have to begin still further back and learn to pray more for himself and for them.

Let all intercessors who are seeking to enter more deeply into their blessed work give a larger place to the ministers, both of their own church and of other churches. Let them plead with God for individual men and for special circles. Let them continue in prayer, so that ministers may be men of power, men of prayer, and men full of the Holy Spirit. Fellow Christians, pray for the ministers!

Our Father who is in heaven, we humbly ask You to arouse believers to a sense of their calling to pray for the ministers of the Gospel in the spirit of faith. Amen.

48

PRAYER FOR ALL BELIEVERS

With all prayer and supplication praying at all seasons in the Spirit, and watching thereunto in all perseverance and supplication for all the saints.
—Ephesians 6:18 RV

Notice how Paul repeated the words in the intensity of his desire to reach the hearts of his readers: *"With all prayer and supplication praying at all seasons...watching thereunto in all perseverance and supplication."* It is *"all prayer...all seasons...all perseverance and supplication."*

Paul felt so deeply the unity of the body of Christ, and he was so sure that that unity could only be realized in the exercise of love and prayer, that he pleaded with the believers at Ephesus to pray unceasingly and fervently for all believers, not only all believers in their immediate circle, but also all believers in all the church of Christ of whom they might hear. Paul knew that unity is strength. As we exercise this power of intercession with all perseverance, we will be delivered from self with all its feeble prayers, and our hearts will be enlarged so that the love of Christ can flow freely and fully through us.

The great lack in true believers often is that, in prayer, they are occupied with themselves and with what God must do for them. Here we have a call to every believer to give himself without ceasing to the exercise of love and prayer. As we forget ourselves, in the faith that God will take charge of us, and as we yield ourselves to the great and blessed work of calling down the blessings of God on our fellowmen, the whole church will be equipped to do its work in making Christ known to every creature. This alone is the healthy and blessed life of a child of God who has yielded himself wholly to Christ Jesus.

Pray for God's children and the church around you. Pray for all the work in which they are engaged, or ought to be. Pray *at all seasons in the Spirit* for all believers. There is no blessedness greater than that of abiding communion with God. And there is no way that leads to the enjoyment of this more surely than the life of intercession for which these words of Paul appeal so pleadingly.

49

MISSIONARY INTERCESSION

Then, having fasted and prayed, and laid hands on them,
they sent them away.
—Acts 13:3

The supreme question of foreign missions is, How do we multiply the number of Christians who will individually and collectively wield this force of intercession for the conversion and transformation of men? Every other consideration and plan is secondary to that of wielding the forces of prayer.

We take for granted that those who love this work and who bear it in their hearts will follow the scriptural command to pray unceasingly for its triumph. With unceasing devotion and intercession, God's people need to approach Him with an attitude that refuses to let God go until He crowns His workers with victory.

Missions has its root in the love of Christ, which was proved on the cross and now lives in our hearts. As men are so earnest in seeking to carry out God's plans for the natural world, so God's children should be at least as wholehearted in seeking to bring Christ's love to all mankind. Intercession is the chief means appointed by God to bring the great redemption within the reach of all.

Pray for missionaries, that the life of Christ may be clear and strong, and that they may be people of prayer, filled with love, people in whom the power of the spiritual life is obvious.

Pray for Christians, that they may know *"the glory of this mystery among the Gentiles* [the unsaved]: *which is Christ in you, the hope of glory"* (Colossians 1:27).

Pray for the teaching of God's Word, that it may be in power. Pray especially for pastors and evangelists, that the Holy Spirit may fill them to be witnesses for Christ among their fellowmen.

Pray, above all, for the church of Christ, that it may be lifted out of its indifference, and that every believer may be brought to understand that the one purpose of his life is to help to make Christ King on the earth.

Our Gracious God, our eyes are focused on You. Will You not in mercy hear our prayers, and by the Holy Spirit reveal the presence and the power of Christ in the work of Your servants? Amen.

THE GRACE OF INTERCESSION

Continue earnestly in prayer, being vigilant in it with
thanksgiving; meanwhile praying also for us.
—Colossians 4:2–3

Nothing can bring us nearer to God and lead us deeper into His love than the work of intercession. Nothing can give us a higher experience of the likeness of God than the power of pouring out our hearts to God in prayer for those around us. Nothing can so closely link us to Jesus Christ, the great Intercessor, and give us the experience of His power and Spirit resting on us, as the yielding of our lives to the work of bringing the great redemption into the hearts and lives of our fellowmen. There is nothing in which we will know more of the powerful working of the Holy Spirit than the prayer breathed by Him into our hearts, *"Abba, Father"* (Mark 14:36), in all the fullness of meaning that it had for Christ at Gethsemane. Nothing can so help us to prove the power and faithfulness of God to His Word, as when we reach out in intercession to the multitudes, either in the church of Christ or in the darkness of heathenism. As we pour out our souls as living sacrifices before God, with the one persistent plea that He will open the windows of heaven and send down His abundant blessings in answer to our pleas, God will be glorified, our souls will reach their highest destiny, and God's kingdom will come.

Nothing will help us to understand and experience the living unity of the body of Christ, and the irresistible power that it can exert, so much as uniting with God's children in the persistent plea that God will arise and have mercy upon Zion (Psalm 102:13), and will make her a light to those who are sitting in darkness (Luke 1:79). My brothers and sisters in Christ, how little we realize what we are losing by not living in fervent intercession! Think of what we will gain for ourselves and for the world if we allow God's Spirit, as a Spirit of grace and of supplication, to master our whole beings!

In heaven, Christ lives to pray (Hebrews 7:25). His whole fellowship with His Father is prayer—an asking and receiving of the fullness of the Spirit for His people. God delights in nothing so much as prayer. Will we not learn to believe that the highest blessings of heaven will be unfolded to us as we pray more?

Blessed Father, pour down the Spirit of supplication and intercession on Your people, for Jesus Christ's sake. Amen.

51

UNITED INTERCESSION

There is one body and one Spirit.
—Ephesians 4:4

Our own bodies teach us how essential it is for every member to seek the welfare of the whole. It is the same in the body of Christ. There are, unfortunately, too many who look upon salvation only in connection with their own happiness. There are also those who know that they do not live for themselves, and they truly seek to bring others to share in their happiness; but they do not yet understand that, in addition to their personal circle or church, they have a calling to include the whole body of Christ Jesus in their love and their intercession.

Yet this is what the Spirit and the love of Christ will enable them to do. Only when intercession for the whole church, by the whole church, ascends to God's throne, can the Spirit of unity and of power have His full influence. The desire that has been awakened for closer union among the different branches of the church of Christ is cause for thanksgiving. And yet the difficulties are so great and, in the case of different nationalities of the world, so apparently insurmountable, that the thought of a united church on earth appears beyond reach.

Let us bless God that there is unity in Christ Jesus, deeper and stronger than any visible manifestation could make it. Let us thank Him that there is a way in which, even now, amid the diversity of denominations, the unity can be practically exemplified and utilized in order to access previously unknown divine strength and blessings in the work of the kingdom. Only in the cultivation and increase of intercession can true unity be realized. As believers are taught what is the meaning of their calling as *a royal priesthood* (1 Peter 2:9), they are led to see that God's love and promises are not confined to their limited spheres of labor. Rather, He invites them to enlarge their hearts, and like Christ—and also like Paul, I might say—to pray for all who believe, or who may still be brought to believe, that this earth and the church of Christ in it will by intercession be bound to the throne of heaven as it has never been before.

Christians and ministers must bind themselves together for this worldwide intercession. This unity will strengthen the confidence that prayer will be heard and that their prayers will become indispensable for the coming of the kingdom.

52

UNCEASING INTERCESSION

Pray without ceasing.
—1 Thessalonians 5:17

How different is the standard of the average Christian, with regard to a life in the service of God, from that which Scripture gives us! In the former the chief thought is personal safety—grace to pardon his sin and to live the kind of life that will secure his entrance into heaven. How high above this is the Bible standard—a Christian surrendering himself with all his powers, with his time, thoughts, and love wholly yielded to the glorious God who has redeemed him! He now delights in serving this God, in whose fellowship heaven is begun.

To the average Christian, the command, *"Pray without ceasing,"* is simply a needless and impossible life of perfection. Who can do it? We can get to heaven without it. To the true believer, on the contrary, it holds out the promise of the highest happiness, of a life crowned by all the blessings that can be brought down on other souls through his intercession. And as he perseveres, unceasing intercession becomes increasingly his highest aim upon earth, his highest joy, his highest experience of the wonderful fellowship with the holy God.

"Pray without ceasing." Let us take hold of these words with a large faith, as a promise of what God's Spirit will work in us, of how close and intimate our union to the Lord Jesus can be, and of our likeness to Him, in His ever blessed intercession at the right

hand of God. Let these words become to us one of the chief elements of our heavenly calling, to be consciously the stewards and administrators of God's grace to the world around us. As we think of how Christ said, *"I in them, and You in Me"* (John 17:23), let us believe that just as the Father worked in Him, so Christ the interceding High Priest will work and pray in us. As the faith of our high calling fills our hearts, we will begin literally to feel that there is nothing on earth for one moment to be compared to the privilege of being God's priests, walking without intermission in His holy presence, bringing the burdens of the souls around us to the footstool of His throne, and receiving at His hands the power and blessing to dispense to our fellowmen.

This is indeed the fulfillment of the Scriptures that say, "Man was created in the likeness and the image of God." (See Genesis 1:26–27.)

53

INTERCESSION: THE LINK BETWEEN HEAVEN AND EARTH

Your will be done on earth as it is in heaven.
—Luke 11:2

When God created heaven and earth, He meant heaven to be the divine pattern to which earth was to be conformed; *"on earth as it is in heaven"* was to be the law of its existence.

This Scripture calls us to think of what constitutes the glory of heaven. God is all in all there. Everything lives in Him and for His glory. As we think of what this earth has now become—with all its sin and misery, with the great majority of people lacking any knowledge of the true God, and with the remainder living only as nominal Christians who are for the greater part utterly indifferent to His claims and are estranged from His holiness and love—we feel what a miracle is needed if these words are to be fulfilled: "*On earth as it is in heaven.*"

How is this ever to come true? Only through the prayers of God's children. Our Lord taught us to pray for it. Intercession is to be the great link between heaven and earth. The intercession of the Son, begun on earth, continued in heaven, and carried on by His redeemed people on earth, will bring about the mighty change—"*on earth as it is in heaven.*" Christ's redeemed ones, who yield themselves fully to His mind and Spirit, make His prayer their own and unceasingly send up the cry, "*Your will be done on earth as it is in heaven.*"

Every prayer of a parent for a child, every prayer of a believer for the saving of the lost or for more grace for those who have been saved, is part of the great unceasing cry going up day and night from this earth: "*On earth as it is in heaven.*"

But when God's children not only learn to pray for their immediate circles and interests, but also enlarge their hearts to take in the whole church and the whole world, then their united supplication will have power with God and will hurry the day when it will indeed be "*on earth as it is in heaven*"—the whole earth filled with the glory of God. Child of God, will you not yield yourself, like Christ, to live with this one prayer: "Father, '*Your will be done on earth as it is in heaven*'"?

54

THE FULFILLMENT OF GOD'S DESIRE

The Lord has chosen Zion; He has desired it for His dwelling place.…Here I will dwell, for I have desired it.
—Psalm 132:13–14

Here you have the one great desire of God that moved Him in the work of redemption. His heart longed for man; He desired to dwell with him and in him.

To Moses He said, *"Let them make Me a sanctuary, that I may dwell among them"* (Exodus 25:8). And just as Israel had to prepare the dwelling for God, His children are now called to yield themselves to God so that He might dwell in them and they might win others to become His habitation. As the desire of God toward us fills our hearts, it will waken within us the desire to gather others around us to become His dwelling, too.

What an honor! What a high calling, to count my worldly business as entirely secondary, and to find my life and my delight in winning souls in whom God may find His heart's delight! *"Here I will dwell, for I have desired it."*

And this is what I can do through intercession. I can pray for those around me, that God would give them His Holy Spirit. God's great plan is that man himself will build Him a habitation. In answer to the unceasing intercession of His children, God will give His power and blessing. As this great desire of God fills us, we will give ourselves wholly to work for its fulfillment.

When David thought of God's desire to dwell in Israel, he said, *"I will not give sleep to my eyes or slumber to my eyelids, until I find a place for the Lord, a dwelling place for the Mighty One of Jacob"* (Psalm 132:4). And since it has been revealed to us what that indwelling of God may be, should we not give our lives for the fulfillment of His heart's desire?

Oh, let us begin, as never before, to pray for our children, for the souls around us, and for all the world—not only because we love them, but especially because God longs for them and gives us the honor of being the channels through whom His blessings are brought down upon them. Children of God, awaken to the realization that God is seeking to train you as intercessors, through whom the great desire of His loving heart can be satisfied!

Oh God, who has said of human hearts, *"Here I will dwell, for I have desired it,"* teach us to pray, day and night, that the desire of Your heart may be fulfilled. Amen.

55

THE FULFILLMENT OF MAN'S DESIRES

Delight yourself also in the Lord, and He shall give you the desires of your heart.
—Psalms 37:4

God is love, an ever flowing fountain out of which streams the unceasing desire to make His creatures the partakers of all the holiness (Hebrews 12:10) and blessedness in Himself. This desire for the salvation of souls is God's perfect will, His highest glory.

To all His children who are willing to yield themselves wholly to Him, God imparts His loving desire to take His place in the hearts of all men. It is in this that the likeness and image of God consist: to have a heart in which His love takes complete possession and leads us to find our highest joy in loving as He does.

It is thus that our text finds its fulfillment: *"Delight yourself also in the LORD"* and in His life of love, *"and He shall give you the desires of your heart."* You can be sure that the intercession of love, rising up to heaven, will be met with the fulfillment of the desires of our hearts. As we delight in what God delights in, such prayer is inspired by God and will have its answer. And our prayer becomes unceasingly, "Your desires, my Father, are mine. Your holy will of love is my will, too."

In fellowship with Him, we acquire the courage to bring our concerns before the Lord in an ever growing confidence that our prayers will be heard. As we reach out in yearning love, we will obtain power to take hold of the will of God to bless. We will also begin to believe that God will work out His own blessed will in giving us the desires of our hearts, because the fulfillment of His desire has been the delight of our souls.

We then become, in the highest sense of the word, God's fellow laborers. Our prayers become part of God's divine work of reaching and saving the lost. And we learn to find our happiness in losing ourselves in the salvation of those around us.

Dear Father, teach us that nothing less than delighting ourselves in You, and in Your desires toward men, can inspire us to pray correctly or can give us the assurance of an answer. Amen.

56

MY GREAT DESIRE

One thing I have desired of the LORD, that will I seek: that I may dwell in the house of the LORD all the days of my life, to behold the beauty of the LORD, and to inquire in His temple.
—Psalm 27:4

Here we have man's response to God's desire to dwell in us. When the desire of God toward us begins to rule our lives and hearts, our desire is fixed on one thing, and that is to dwell in the house of the Lord all the days of our lives, to behold the beauty of the Lord, to worship Him in the beauty of holiness, and then to inquire in His temple and to learn what He meant when He said, *"I, the LORD, have spoken it, and I will do it....I will also let the house of Israel inquire of Me to do this for them"* (Ezekiel 36:36–37).

The more we realize the desire of God's love to put His rest in our hearts, and the more we desire to dwell every day in His temple and to behold His beauty, the more the Spirit of intercession will grow upon us, to claim all that God has promised in His new covenant. Whether we think of our church or country, of our home or school, of people close to us or far away; whether we think of the saved and all their needs or the unsaved and their danger, the thought that God is longing to find His home and His rest in the hearts of men, if we only *"inquire"* of Him, will rouse us entirely. All the thoughts of our feebleness and unworthiness will be swallowed up in the wonderful assurance that He has said of human hearts, *"This is My resting place forever; here I will dwell, for I have desired it"* (Psalm 132:14).

As we see by faith how high our calling is, how indispensable God has made fervent, intense, persistent prayer as the condition of His purpose being fulfilled, we will be drawn to give up our lives to a closer walk with God, to an unceasing waiting upon Him, and to a testimony to our fellowmen of what God will do in them and in us.

Is it not wonderful beyond all thought, this divine partnership in which God commits the fulfillment of His desires to our keeping? We should be utterly ashamed that we have so little realized it!

Our Father in heaven, we ask that You would give, give in power, the Spirit of grace and supplication to Your people, for Jesus's sake. Amen.

57

INTERCESSION DAY AND NIGHT

Shall God not avenge His own elect who cry out day and night to Him, though He bears long with them?
—Luke 18:7

When Nehemiah heard of the destruction of Jerusalem, he cried to God, "*Hear the prayer of Your servant which I pray before You now, day and night*" (Nehemiah 1:6). Concerning the watchman set on the walls of Jerusalem, God said, "*They shall never hold their peace day or night*" (Isaiah 62:6). And Paul wrote, "*Night and day praying exceedingly…that He may establish your hearts blameless in holiness before our God and Father"* (1 Thessalonians 3:10, 13).

Is such prayer really needed and really possible? Yes. It is needed when the heart is so entirely possessed by some desire that it cannot rest until the desire is fulfilled. And it is possible when one's life has so come under the power of the heavenly blessing to such a degree that nothing can keep it from sacrificing all to obtain it.

When a child of God begins to get a real vision into the need of the church and of the world—a vision of the divine redemption that God has promised in the outpouring of His love into our hearts, a vision of the power of true intercession to bring down the heavenly blessing, and a vision of the honor of being allowed as intercessors to take part in that work—it naturally follows that he regards as the most heavenly thing upon earth his work of crying day and night to God for the revelation of His mighty power.

Let us learn from David, who said, *"Zeal for Your house has eaten me up"* (Psalm 69:9). Let us learn from Christ our Lord, of whom these words were so intensely true. There is nothing so much worth living for as satisfying the heart of God in His longing for human fellowship and affection, and winning hearts to be His dwelling places. How can we rest until we have found a place for the Mighty One in our hearts and have yielded ourselves to the great work of intercession for so many after whom the desires of God are going out?

God, grant that our hearts may be so brought under the influence of these divine truths that we will yield ourselves in pure devotion to Christ. May our longing to satisfy Your heart be the chief aim of our lives. Lord Jesus, the great Intercessor, breathe Your own Spirit into our hearts, for Your name's sake. Amen.

58

THE HIGH PRIEST AND HIS INTERCESSION

We have such a High Priest…[who is] able to save to the
uttermost those who come to God through Him, since He
always lives to make intercession for them.
—Hebrews 8:1; 7:25

In Israel, what a difference there was between the high priest and the priests and Levites! The high priest alone had access to the Holiest of All. He bore on his forehead the golden crown, "HOLINESS TO THE LORD" (Exodus 28:36), and by his intercession on the great Day of Atonement he bore the sins of the people. The priests, in contrast, brought the daily sacrifices, stood before the Lord, and came out to bless the people. Though the difference between high priest and priest was great, their unity was even greater. The priests formed one body with the high priest, sharing with him the power to appear before God to receive and dispense His blessings to His people.

It is the same with our great High Priest. Jesus alone has power with God, in a never ceasing intercession, to obtain from the Father what His people need. Though there is infinite distance between Him and the *"royal priesthood"* (1 Peter 2:9) that surrounds Him for His service, the unity and the fellowship into which His people have been taken up with Him is no less infinite. When He obtains blessings from His Father for us, He holds them so that His people may receive from Him through their fervent supplication.

As long as Christians simply think of being saved, and of a life that will make that salvation secure, they will never understand the mystery of the power of intercession to which they are called.

But once they see that salvation means a vital union with Jesus Christ—an actual sharing of His life dwelling and working in us, and the consecration of our whole beings to live and labor, to think and will, and to find our highest joy in living as a royal priesthood—the church will "put on her strength" (see Isaiah 52:1) and will prove, in fellowship with God and man, how truly the likeness and the power of Christ dwell in her.

Oh, that God would open our hearts to know what our royal priesthood is and what the real meaning is of our living and praying in the name of Jesus, so that what we ask will indeed be given to us!

Lord Jesus, our holy High Priest, breathe the spirit of Your own holy priesthood into our hearts. Amen.

59

A ROYAL PRIESTHOOD

Call to Me, and I will answer you, and show you great and mighty things, which you do not know.
—Jeremiah 33:3

As you ask God for the great mercies of the new covenant to be bestowed, keep the following thoughts in mind.

1. *The infinite willingness of God to bless.* His very nature is a pledge of it. *"He delights in mercy"* (Micah 7:18). He waits to be gracious. His promises and the experience of His saints assure us of it.

2. *Why the blessing so often tarries.* In creating man with a free will, and in making him a partner in the rule of the earth, God limited Himself. He made Himself dependent on what man would do. Man's prayer would hold the measure of what God could do in blessing.

3. *God is hindered and disappointed when His children do not pray, or pray very little.* The low, feeble life of the church, the lack of the power of the Holy Spirit for conversion and holiness, is all owing to the lack of prayer. How different the state of the church and of the world would be if God's people were to take no rest in calling upon Him!

4. *Yet God has blessed, just up to the measure of the faith and the zeal of His people.* They should never be content with this as a sign of His approval. Rather, they should say, "If God has thus blessed our feeble efforts and prayers, what will He not do if we yield ourselves wholly to a life of intercession?"

5. *What a call to penitence and confession that our lack of consecration has kept back God's blessing from the world!* He was ready to save men, but we were not willing for the sacrifice of a wholehearted devotion to Christ and His service.

Dear readers, God depends on you to take your place before His throne as intercessors. Awake to your holy calling as *"a royal priesthood"* (1 Peter 2:9). Begin to live a new life in the assurance that intercession, in fellowship with the interceding Lord Jesus in heaven, is the highest privilege a man can desire. In this spirit, hold this near to your heart: *"Call to Me, and I will answer you, and show you great and mighty things, which you do not know."*

Are you not willing—do you not desire supremely—to give yourself wholly to this blessed calling, and in the power of Jesus Christ to make intercession for God's church and people, and for a dying world, the one chief aim of your life? Is this asking too much? Is it too much to yield your life for this holy service of the royal priesthood, to that blessed Lord who gave Himself for us?

60

INTERCESSION: A DIVINE REALITY

Then another angel…came…[and] he was given much incense, that he should offer it with the prayers of all the saints upon the golden altar which was before the throne.
—Revelation 8:3

Intercession is, by amazing grace, an essential element in God's redeeming purpose—to such a degree that, without it, the failure of its accomplishment may lie at our door. Christ's intercession in heaven is essential to His carrying out the work He began on earth, but He calls for the intercession of the saints in the attainment of His purpose. Just think of what we read: *"All things are of God, who has reconciled us to Himself through Jesus Christ, and has given us the ministry of reconciliation"* (2 Corinthians 5:18). As the reconciliation was dependent on Christ's doing His part, so in the accomplishment of the work He calls on the church to do her part. Paul regarded unceasing intercession as indispensable to the fulfillment of the work that had been entrusted to him. It is just one aspect of the mighty power of God that works in the hearts of His believing people.

Intercession is indeed a divine reality. Without it, the church loses one of its chief beauties, loses the joy and the power of the Spirit life for achieving great things for God. Without it, the command to preach the Gospel to every creature can never be carried out. Without it, there is no power for the church to recover from her sickly, feeble life and to conquer the world. And in the life of the believer, there can be no entrance into the abundant life and joy of daily fellowship with God unless he takes his place among God's elect—the watchmen and remembrancers of God who cry to Him *"day and night"* (Luke 18:7).

Church of Christ, awaken! Listen to the call: *"Pray without ceasing"* (1 Thessalonians 5:17). Take no rest, and give God no rest. Even though it may be with a sigh from the depths of the heart, let the answer be, *"For Zion's sake I will not hold My peace"* (Isaiah 62:1). God's Spirit will reveal to us the power of a life of intercession as a divine reality, an essential and indispensable element of the great redemption and therefore also of the true Christian life.

May God help us to know and fulfill our calling!

61

TRUE WORSHIP

Keep the words of this book. Worship God.
—Revelation 22:9

Undoubtedly, many readers have asked more than once, "What is the reason that prayer and intercession are not a greater joy and delight to Christians? Is there any way in which we may be more inclined to make fellowship with God our chief joy, and as intercessors to bring down His power and blessing on those for whom we pray?"

There may be more than one answer to these questions. But the chief answer is undoubtedly, We know God too little. In our prayers, our hearts are not set chiefly on waiting for His presence. And yet it should be so. We think mostly of ourselves, our needs and weaknesses, our desires and prayers. But we forget that in every prayer God must be first, must be all. To seek Him, to find Him, to wait in His presence, to be assured that His holy presence rests upon us, that He actually listens to what we say and is working in us—this alone gives the inspiration that makes prayer as natural and easy to us as the fellowship of a child with his father.

How is one to reach this nearness to God and fellowship with Him? The answer is simple: we must give God time to make Himself known to us. Believe with all your heart that, just as you present yourself to God in prayer, so God presents Himself to you as the Hearer of prayer. But you cannot realize this unless you give Him time and quiet. It is not the volume or the earnestness of your words in which prayer has its power, but in the living faith that God Himself is taking you and your prayer into His loving heart. He Himself will give the assurance that, in His time, your prayer will be heard.

Learn how to meet God in every prayer. I give you Scriptures with which your heart can bow before God, waiting on Him to make them living and true in your experience.

Begin today with this verse: *"To You, O Lord, I lift up my soul"* (Psalm 25:1). Bow before Him in stillness, believing that He looks on you and will reveal His presence.

My soul thirsts for God, for the living God.   (Psalm 42:2)

62

GOD IS A SPIRIT

*God is Spirit, and those who worship Him
must worship in spirit and truth.*
—John 4:24

When God created man and breathed into him His own spirit, man became a living soul. The soul stood midway between the spirit and the body, to yield either to the spirit to be lifted up to God, or to the flesh and its lusts. In the fall, man refused to listen to his own spirit, and so it became the slave of the body. The spirit in man became utterly darkened.

In regeneration, it is this spirit that is quickened and born again from above. In the regenerated life and in fellowship with God, it is the spirit of man that must continually yield itself to the Spirit of God. Man's spirit is the deepest inward part of the human being. The Scriptures read, *"You desire truth in the inward parts, and in the hidden part You will make me to know wisdom"* (Psalm 51:6), and *"I will put my law in their inward parts"* (Jeremiah 31:33 KJV). Also concerning this, Isaiah said, *"With my soul I have desired You in the night, yes, by my spirit within me I will seek You early"* (Isaiah 26:9). The soul must sink down into the depths of the hidden spirit and must stir itself to seek God.

God is a Spirit, most holy and most glorious. He gave us a spirit with the one purpose of holding fellowship with Himself. Through sin, that purpose has been darkened and nearly quenched. There is no way for it to be restored except by presenting the soul in stillness before God for the working of His Holy Spirit in our spirits. Deeper than our thoughts and feelings, God will in our inward parts, in our spirits within us, teach us to worship Him "*in spirit and truth.*"

"*The Father is seeking such to worship Him*" (John 4:23). He Himself by the Holy Spirit will teach us this if we wait upon Him. In this quiet hour, be still before God, and yield yourself with your whole heart to believe in and to receive the gentle working of His Spirit. And breathe out such words as these: "*With my soul I have desired You in the night, yes, by my spirit within me I will seek You early*" (Isaiah 26:9); "*On You I wait all the day*" (Psalm 25:5).

63

INTERCESSION AND ADORATION

Worship the LORD in the beauty of holiness!
—Psalm 96:9

The better we know God, the more wonderful our insight into the power of intercession becomes. We begin to understand that it is the great means by which man can take part in the carrying out of God's purpose. God has commissioned His people to make known and communicate to men the whole plan of redemption through Christ. In all this, intercession is the chief and essential element, because in it His servants enter into the full fellowship with Christ, and they receive the power of the Spirit and of heaven as their power for service.

It is easy to see why God has so ordered it. He desires to renew us after His image and likeness. And there is no other way to do this but by our making His desires our own, so that we breathe His character; and by sacrificing ourselves in love, so that we may become to some degree like Christ, ever living to make intercession (Hebrews 7:25). Such can be the life of the consecrated believer.

The clearer one's insight into this great purpose of God, the more the need will be felt to enter very truly into God's presence in the spirit of humble worship and holy adoration. The more we take time to abide in God's presence, to enter fully into His mind and will, to get our whole souls possessed by the thought of His glorious purpose, the stronger our faith will become that God will Himself work out all the good pleasure of His will (Philippians 2:13) through our prayers. As the glory of God shines upon us, we will become conscious of the depths of our helplessness, and so we will rise up into the faith that believes that God will do *above all that we ask or think*" (Ephesians 3:20).

Intercession will lead us to feel the need for a deeper adoration. Adoration will give new power for intercession. A true intercession and a deeper adoration will always be inseparable.

The secret of true adoration can only be known by the individual who spends time waiting in God's presence, yielding to God so that He may reveal Himself. Adoration will indeed equip us for the great work of making God's glory known.

> Oh come, let us worship and bow down; let us kneel before the LORD our Maker. For He is our God.   (Psalm 95:6–7)

> Give to the LORD the glory due His name.
> (1 Chronicles 16:29)

64

THE DESIRE FOR GOD

With my soul I have desired You in the night.
—Isaiah 26:9

What is the chief thing, the greatest and most glorious, that man can see or find upon earth? Nothing less than God Himself.

And what is the chief, the best, the most glorious thing that a man can and needs to do every day? Nothing less than to seek, to know, to love, and to praise this glorious God. As glorious as God is, so is the glory that begins to work in the heart and life of the man who gives himself to live for God.

My brother or sister in Christ, have you learned the first and greatest thing you have to do every day? Nothing less and nothing greater than to seek this God, to meet Him, to worship Him, to live for Him and for His glory. It is a great step in the life of a Christian when he truly sees this truth and yields himself to consider fellowship with God every day as the chief purpose of his life.

Take time and ask whether this is not the highest wisdom, and the one thing for which a Christian is to live above all—to know his God rightly, and to love Him with his whole heart. Believe not only that it is true, but also that God's greatest desire is for you to live thus with Him. In answer to prayer, He will indeed enable you to do so.

Begin today, and take a word from God's Book to speak to Him in the stillness of your soul: *"O God, You are my God; early*

101

will I seek You; my soul thirsts for You; my flesh longs for You....My soul follows close behind You" (Psalm 63:1, 8); *"With my whole heart I have sought You"* (Psalm 119:10).

Repeat these words in deep reverence and childlike longing until their spirit and power enter your heart. Then wait upon God until you begin to realize the blessedness of meeting with Him in this way. As you persevere, you will learn to expect that the fear and the presence of God can abide with you throughout the day.

I waited patiently for the LORD; and He inclined to me, and heard my cry. (Psalm 40:1)

65

SILENT ADORATION

My soul silently waits for God....My soul, wait silently for God alone, for my expectation is from Him.
—Psalm 62:1, 5

When man in his littleness and God in His glory meet, we all understand that what God says has infinitely more worth than what man says. Yet our prayers so often consist of telling God what we need that we give Him no time to speak to us. Our prayers are often so indefinite and vague. It is a great lesson to learn, that to be silent before God is the secret of true adoration. Let us remember the promise:

In quietness and confidence shall be your strength.
(Isaiah 30:15)

I wait for the LORD, *my soul waits, and in His word I do hope.* (Psalm 130:5)

As the soul bows itself before Him to remember His greatness, His holiness, His power, and His love, and as it seeks to give Him the honor, reverence, and worship that are His due, the heart will be opened to receive the divine impression of the nearness of God and of the working of His power.

Oh Christian, believe that such worship of God—in which you bow lower and lower in your nothingness, and in which you lift up your thoughts to realize God's presence as He gives Himself to you in Christ Jesus—is the sure way to give Him the glory that is His due and to lead to the highest blessedness that can be found in prayer.

Do not imagine that such worship is time lost. Do not turn from it if at first it appears difficult or fruitless. Be assured that it brings you into the right relation to God. It opens the way to fellowship with Him. It leads to the blessed assurance that He is looking on you in tender love and is working in you with a secret but divine power. As you become more accustomed to it, it will give you the sense of His presence abiding with you all day long. It will make you strong to testify for God. Men will begin to feel that you have been with God. Someone has said, "No one is able to influence others for goodness and holiness beyond the amount of God that is in him."

But the LORD *is in His holy temple. Let all the earth keep silence before Him.* (Habakkuk 2:20)

Be silent, all flesh, before the LORD, *for He is aroused from His holy habitation!* (Zechariah 2:13)

THE LIGHT OF GOD'S COUNTENANCE

God is light and in Him is no darkness at all.
—1 John 1:5

The LORD is my light.
—Psalm 27:1

Every morning the sun rises, and we walk in its light and perform our daily duties with gladness. Whether we think of it or not, the light of the sun shines on us all day.

Every morning the light of God shines upon His children. But in order to enjoy the light of God's countenance, the soul must turn to God and trust Him to let His light shine upon it.

When there is a shipwreck at midnight, with what longing the sailors look for the morning! How often the sigh goes up, "When will the day break?" Similarly, the Christian must wait on God and rest patiently until His light shines upon him.

My soul waits for the Lord more than those who watch for the morning. (Psalm 130:6)

Dear reader, begin each day with one of these prayers:

Make Your face shine upon Your servant. (Psalm 31:16)

LORD, lift up the light of Your countenance upon us.
(Psalm 4:6)

Cause Your face to shine, and we shall be saved!

(Psalm 80:3)

Do not rest until you know that the light of His countenance and His blessing is resting on you. Then you will experience the truth of these words: *"They walk...in the light of Your countenance. In Your name they rejoice all day long"* (Psalm 89:15–16).

Children of God, believe that it is the ardent longing of your Father that you should dwell and rejoice in His light all day long. Just as you need the light of the sun each hour, so the heavenly light, the light of the Father, is indispensable. As surely as we receive and enjoy the light of the sun, so we may confidently know that God is longing to let His light shine on us.

Even when there are clouds, we still have the sun. In the midst of difficulties, the light of God will rest upon you without ceasing. If you are sure that the sun has risen, you count on its light all day. Make sure that the light of God shines upon you in the morning, and you can count on that light being with you all day long.

Do not rest until you have said, *"There are many who say, 'Who will show us any good?' Lord, lift up the light of Your countenance upon us"* (Psalm 4:6). Take time, until that light shines in your heart, and you can truly say, *"The Lord is my light."*

67

FAITH IN GOD

So Jesus answered and said to them, "Have faith in God."
—Mark 11:22

As the eye is the organ by which we see the light and rejoice in it, so faith is the power by which we see the light of God and walk in it.

Man was made for God, in His likeness; his whole being was formed according to the divine pattern. Just think of man's wonderful power of discovering all the thoughts of God hidden in nature. Think of the heart, with its unlimited powers of selfsacrifice and love. Man was made for God, to seek Him, to find Him, to grow up into His likeness, and to show forth His glory—in the fullest sense, to be His dwelling. And faith is the eye that, turning away from the world and self, looks up to God and sees light in His light. To the man of faith, God reveals Himself.

How often we toil and try to waken thoughts and feelings concerning God, which are but a faint shadow, and we forget to gaze on the God who is the Incomparable Original! If only we could realize that God reveals Himself in the depths of our souls!

"Without faith it is impossible to please [God]*"* (Hebrews 11:6) or to know Him. In our quiet time, we have to pray to our *"Father who is in the secret place"* (Matthew 6:6). There He hides us *"in the secret place of His tabernacle"* (Psalm 27:5). And there, as we wait and worship before Him, He will let His light shine into our hearts.

Let your one desire be to take time and be still before God, believing with an unbounded faith in His longing to make Himself known to you. Feed on God's Word, to make you strong in faith. Let that faith extend itself to think of what God's glory is, of what His power is to reveal Himself to you, and of what His longing love is to get complete possession of you.

Such faith, exercised and strengthened day by day in secret fellowship with God, will become the habit of our lives, keeping us ever in the enjoyment of His presence and the experience of His saving power.

Abraham *"was strengthened in faith, giving glory to God, and being fully convinced that what He had promised He was also able to perform"* (Romans 4:20–21).

I believe God that it will be just as it was told me.

(Acts 27:25)

Wait on the Lord; be of good courage, and He shall strengthen your heart; wait, I say, on the Lord! (Psalm 27:14)

68

ALONE WITH GOD

And it happened, as He was alone praying.
—Luke 9:18

He departed again to the mountain by Himself alone.
—John 6:15

Man needs to be alone with God. Man fell when, through the lust of the flesh and the world, he was brought under the power of things visible and earthly. His restoration is meant to bring him back to the Father's house, the Father's presence, the Father's love and fellowship. Salvation means being brought to love and to delight in the presence of God.

Man needs to be alone with God. Without this, God cannot have the opportunity to shine into his heart, to transform his nature by His divine working, to take possession of him, and to fill him with His fullness.

Man needs to be alone with God, to yield to the presence and power of His holiness, of His life, and of His love. Christ on earth needed it; He could not live the life of a Son here in the flesh without at times separating Himself entirely from His surroundings and being alone with God. How much more must this be indispensable to us!

When our Lord Jesus gave us the blessed command to enter our inner chamber and shut the door in order to pray to our Father in secret, He gave us the promise that the Father would hear such prayers and would mightily answer them in our lives before men. (See Matthew 6:4.)

Alone with God—that is the secret of true prayer, of true power in prayer, of real living, of facetoface fellowship with God, and of power for service. There is no true, deep conversion; no true, deep holiness; no clothing with the Holy Spirit and with power; no abiding peace or joy, without being daily alone with God. As someone has said, "There is no path to holiness, but in being much and long alone with God."

The institution of daily, secret prayer is an inestimable privilege. Let it be the one thing our hearts are set on: seeking, finding, and meeting God. Take time to be alone with God. The time will come when you will be amazed at the thought that one could suggest that five minutes was enough.

> *Give heed to the voice of my cry, my King and my God, for to You I will pray. My voice You shall hear in the morning, O LORD; in the morning I will direct it to You, and I will look up.* (Psalm 5:2–3)

WHOLLY FOR GOD

Whom have I in heaven but You? And there is none upon
earth that I desire besides You.
—Psalm 73:25

Alone with God—this is a lesson of the deepest importance. May we seek grace from God to reach its depths. Then we will learn that there is another lesson of equally deep significance: wholly for God.

As we find that it is not easy to persevere in being alone with God, we begin to see that it is because the other is lacking; we are not "wholly for God." Because He is the only God and is alone the Adorable One, God has a right to demand to have us wholly for Himself. Without this surrender, He cannot make His power known. We read in the Old Testament that His servants, Abraham, Moses, Elijah, and David, gave themselves wholly and unreservedly to God, so that He could work out His plans through them. It is only the fully surrendered heart that can fully trust God for all He has promised.

This world teaches us that if anyone desires to do a great work, he must give himself wholly to it. This law is especially true of the love of a mother for her child. She gives herself wholly to the little one whom she loves. Is it not reasonable that the great God of love should have us wholly for Himself? And will we not take the words *wholly for God* as the keynote for our devotions every morning when we awaken? Just as God gives Himself wholly to us, so does He desire that we give ourselves wholly to Him.

In the inner chamber, let us meditate on these things alone with God, and with earnest desire ask Him by His almighty power to work in us all that is pleasing in His sight.

Wholly for God—what a privilege! What wonderful grace prepares us for it! Wholly for God—separated from men, from work, and from all that might draw us away—what great blessedness as the soul learns what it means, and what God gives with it!

You shall love the LORD your God with all your heart, with all your soul, and with all your mind. (Matthew 22:37)

[They] sought Him with all their soul; and He was found by them. (2 Chronicles 15:15)

With my whole heart I have sought You. (Psalm 119:10)

70

THE KNOWLEDGE OF GOD

This is eternal life, that they may know You.
—John 17:3

The knowledge of God is absolutely necessary for the spiritual life. It is eternal life. It is not the intellectual knowledge we receive from others, or through our own powers of thought, but the living, experiential knowledge in which God makes Himself known to the soul. Just as the rays of the sun on a cold winter's day warm the body, imparting its heat to us, so the living God sheds the lifegiving rays of His holiness and love into the heart of one who waits on Him.

Why do we so seldom experience this lifegiving power of the true knowledge of God? Because we do not give God enough time to reveal Himself to us. When we pray, we think we know well enough how to speak to God. And we forget that one of the very first things in prayer is to be silent before God, so that He may reveal Himself. By His hidden but mighty power, God will manifest His presence, resting on us and working in us. To know God in the personal experience of His presence and love is life indeed.

Brother Lawrence, author of *The Practice of the Presence of God*, had a great longing to know God, and for this purpose went into a monastery. His spiritual advisers gave him prayer books to use, but he put them aside. "It helps little to pray," he said, "if I do not know the God to whom I pray." And he believed that God would reveal Himself. Brother Lawrence remained in silent adoration for a long time, in order to come under the full impression of the presence of this great and holy Being. He continued in this practice until, later, he lived consciously and constantly in God's presence and experienced His blessed nearness and keeping power. Just as the sun rising each morning is the pledge of light throughout the day, so the quiet time of waiting upon God, yielding ourselves for Him to shine on us, will be the pledge of His presence and His power abiding with us all day long. Be sure that the Sun has risen upon your soul.

Learn this great lesson: as the sun on a cold day shines on us and imparts its warmth, believe that the living God will work in you with His love and His almighty power. God will reveal Himself as life and light and joy and strength to the soul who waits upon Him.

> Lord, *lift up the light of Your countenance upon us.*
>
> (Psalm 4:6)

> Be still, and know that I am God. (Psalm 46:10)

71

GOD THE FATHER

Baptizing them in the name of the Father and of the Son and of the Holy Spirit.
—Matthew 28:19

We will do well to remember that the doctrine of the Holy Trinity has a deep devotional aspect. As we think of God, we remember the inconceivable distance that separates Him in His holiness from sinful men, and we bow in deep contrition and holy fear. As we think of Christ the Son, we remember the inconceivable nearness in which He came to be born of a woman, a daughter of Adam, and to die the accursed death, and so to be inseparably joined to us for all eternity. And as we think of the Holy Spirit, we remember the inconceivable blessedness of God having His abode in us, and making us His home and His temple throughout eternity.

When Christ taught us to say, *"Our Father in heaven"* (Matthew 6:9), He immediately added, *"Hallowed be Your name"* (v. 9). As God is holy, so we are to be holy, too. And there is no way of becoming holy but by considering His name most holy and drawing near to Him in prayer.

How often we speak His name without any sense of the unspeakable privilege of our relationship with God! If we would just take time to come into contact with God and to worship Him in His love, how the inner chamber would become to us the gate of heaven!

Child of God, if you pray to your Father in secret, bow very low before Him, and seek to adore His name as most holy. Remember that this is the highest blessedness of prayer.

Pray to your Father who is in the secret place; and your Father who sees in secret will reward you openly. (Matthew 6:6)

What an unspeakable privilege, to be alone with God in secret and to say, "My Father!" How incredible to have the assurance that He has indeed seen me in secret and will reward me openly. Take time until you can say, *"I have seen God face to face, and my life is preserved"* (Genesis 32:30).

72

GOD THE SON

*Grace to you and peace from God our Father
and the Lord Jesus Christ.*
—Romans 1:7

It is remarkable that the apostle Paul in each of his thirteen epistles wrote: *"Grace to you and peace from God our Father and the Lord Jesus Christ."* He had such a deep sense of the inseparable oneness of the Father and the Son in the work of grace, that in each opening benediction he referred to both.

This is a lesson of the utmost importance for us. There may be times in the Christian life when we think chiefly of God the Father, and so pray only to Him. But later on, we realize that it may cause spiritual loss if we do not grasp the truth that each day and each hour it is only through faith in Christ and in being united with Him that we can enjoy a full and abiding fellowship with God.

Remember what we read of the Lamb in the midst of the throne. John had seen One sitting on a throne. *"The four living creatures…do not rest day or night, saying: 'Holy, holy, holy, Lord God Almighty, who was and is and is to come!'"* (Revelation 4:8).

Later, John saw *"in the midst of the throne…a Lamb as though it had been slain"* (Revelation 5:6). Of all the worshipping multitude, none could see God without first seeing Christ the Lamb of God. And none could see Christ without seeing the glory of God, the Father and Son inseparably One.

Oh Christian, if you wish to know and worship God fully, seek Him and worship Him in Christ. And if you seek Christ, seek Him and worship Him in God. Then you will understand what it means to have *"your life…hidden with Christ in God"* (Colossians 3:3), and your experience will be that the fellowship and adoration of Christ is indispensable to the full knowledge of the love and holiness of God.

Be still, and speak these words in deepest reverence: *"Grace… and peace"*—all I can desire—*"from God our Father and the Lord Jesus Christ."*

Take time to meditate on this, to believe and to expect all from God the Father who sits upon the throne, and from the Lord Jesus Christ, the Lamb in the midst of the throne. Then you will learn to truly worship God. Return frequently to this sacred scene, to give *"glory…to Him who sits on the throne, and to the Lamb"* (Revelation 5:13).

73

GOD THE HOLY SPIRIT

*For through Him we both have access by
one Spirit to the Father.*
—Ephesians 2:18

In our communion with God in the inner chamber, we must guard against the danger of seeking to know God and Christ in the power of the intellect or the emotions. The Holy Spirit has been given for the sole purpose that *"through Him we…have access by one Spirit to the Father."* Let us beware, lest all our labor be in vain because we do not wait for the teaching of the Spirit.

Christ taught His disciples this truth on His last night. Speaking of the coming of the Comforter, He said, *"In that day you will ask…the Father in My name….Ask, and you will receive, that your joy may be full"* (John 16:23–24). Take hold of the truth that the Holy Spirit was given with the one great purpose of teaching us to pray. He makes the fellowship with the Father and the Son a blessed reality. Be strong in the faith that He is working secretly in you. As you enter the inner chamber, give yourself wholly to His guidance as your Teacher in all your intercession and adoration.

When Christ said to the disciples on the evening of the Resurrection, *"Receive the Holy Spirit"* (John 20:22), it was, for one thing, to strengthen and equip them for the ten days of prayer and for their receiving the fullness of the Spirit. This suggests to us three things we ought to remember when we draw near to God in prayer:

1. *We must pray in the confidence that the Holy Spirit dwells in us.* And we must yield ourselves definitely, in stillness of soul, to His leading. Take time for this.

2. *We must believe that the "greater works" (John 5:20) of the Spirit will be given in answer to prayer.* Such "works" bring us toward the enlightening and strengthening of the spiritual life, toward the fullness of the Spirit.

3. *We must believe that through the Spirit, in unity with all God's children, we may ask and expect the mighty workings of that Spirit on His church and people.*

He who believes in Me, as the Scripture has said, out of his heart will flow rivers of living water.　　　　(John 7:38)

Do you believe this?　　　　　　　　　　(John 11:26)

74

THE SECRET OF THE LORD

Go into your room, and when you have shut your door, pray to your Father who is in the secret place; and your Father who sees in secret will reward you openly.
—Matthew 6:6

Christ greatly desired that His disciples would know God as their Father, and that they would have secret fellowship with Him. In His own life, He found it not only indispensable, but also the highest happiness to meet the Father in secret. And He wants us to realize that it is impossible to be true, wholehearted disciples without daily fellowship with the Father in heaven, who waits for us "*in secret.*"

God is a God who hides Himself from the world and all that is of the world. He wants to draw us away from the world and from ourselves. Instead, He offers us the blessedness of close, intimate communion with Himself. Oh, that God's children would understand this!

Believers enjoyed this experience in Old Testament times: "*You are my hiding place*" (Psalm 32:7); "*He who dwells in the secret place of the Most High shall abide under the shadow of the Almighty*" (Psalm 91:1); "*The secret of the Lord is with those who fear Him*" (Psalm 25:14). How much more Christians in the new covenant ought to value this secret fellowship with God! We read: "*Ye are dead, and your life is hid with Christ in God*" (Colossians 3:3 KJV). If we really believe this, we will have the joyful assurance that our lives, hidden "*with Christ in God*" in such divine keeping, are safe and beyond the reach of every foe. We should confidently and daily seek the renewal of our spiritual lives in prayer to our Father who is "*in secret.*"

Because we are dead with Christ, because we are one with Him in the likeness of His death and of His resurrection, we know that, as the roots of a tree are hidden under the earth, so the roots of our daily lives are hidden deep in God.

O soul, take time to realize: "*You shall hide* [me] *in the secret place of Your presence*" (Psalm 31:20).

Our first thought in prayer should be, "I must know that I am alone with God, and that God is with me."

In the secret place of His tabernacle He shall hide me.
(Psalm 27:5)

HALF AN HOUR OF SILENCE IN HEAVEN

There was silence in heaven for about half an hour....
Then another angel...came and stood at the altar.
He was given much incense, that he should offer it with the
prayers of all the saints upon the golden altar which was
before the throne. And the smoke of the incense,
with the prayers of the saints, ascended before God.
—Revelation 8:1, 3–4

*T*here was silence in heaven for about half an hour," to bring the prayers of the saints before God, before the first angel sounded his trumpet. Tens of thousands of God's children have felt the absolute need for silence and detachment from the things of earth for half an hour, in order to present their prayers before God, and in fellowship with Him to be strengthened for their daily work.

How often the complaint is heard that there is no time for prayer! Very often the confession is made that, even if time could be found, one feels unable to spend the time in real fellowship with God. No one needs to ask what it is that hinders growth in the spiritual life. The secret of strength can only be found in living communion with God.

Oh dear Christian, if you would only obey Christ when He says, *"When you have shut your door, pray to your Father who is in the secret place"* (Matthew 6:6)! If you would only have the courage to be alone with God for half an hour! Do not think to yourself, "I will not know how to spend the time." Just believe that if you begin and are faithful, bowing in silence before God, He will reveal Himself to you.

If you need help, read some passage of Scripture and let God's Word speak to you. Then bow in deepest humility before God, and wait on Him. He will work within you. Read Psalm 61, 62, or 63, and speak the words out before God. Then begin to pray. Intercede for your own household and children, for the congregation, for the church and minister, for schools and missions. Continue praying, though the time may seem long. God will reward you. But above all, be sure you meet God.

God desires to bless you. Is it not worth the trouble to spend half an hour alone with God? In heaven itself, there was need for half an hour's silence to present the prayers of the saints before God. If you persevere, you may find that the half hour that seems the most difficult in the whole day may eventually become the most blessed in your whole life.

My soul, wait silently for God alone, for my expectation is from Him.   (Psalm 62:5)

76

GOD'S GREATNESS

You are great, and do wondrous things; You alone are God.
—Psalm 86:10

When anyone begins an important work, he takes time and gives his attention to consider the greatness of his undertaking.

Scientists, in studying nature, require years of labor to grasp the magnitude of, for instance, the sun, the stars, and the planets. Is not our glorious God worthy that we should take time to know and adore His greatness?

Yet how superficial is our knowledge of God's greatness! We do not allow ourselves time to bow before Him and to come under the deep impression of His incomprehensible majesty and glory.

Meditate on the following Scriptures until you are filled with some sense of what a glorious being God is: *"Great is the* LORD, *and greatly to be praised; and His greatness is unsearchable"* (Psalm 145:3); *"I will declare Your greatness. They shall utter the memory of Your great goodness"* (vv. 6–7).

Do not imagine that it is easy to grasp the meaning of these words. Take time for them to master your heart, until you bow in what may be speechless adoration before God.

"Ah, Lord GOD!...*There is nothing too hard for You...the Great, the Mighty God....You are great in counsel and mighty in work"* (Jeremiah 32:17–19). To this God answers, *"Behold, I am the* LORD, *the God of all flesh. Is there anything too hard for Me?"* (v. 27).

The right understanding of God's greatness will take time. But if we give God the honor that is His due, and if our faith grows strong in the knowledge of what a great and powerful God we have, we will be led to wait in the inner chamber, to bow in humble worship before this great and mighty God. In His abundant mercy, He will teach us through the Holy Spirit to say, *"The* LORD *is the great God, and the great King above all gods....Oh come, let us worship and bow down; let us kneel before the* LORD *our Maker"* (Psalm 95:3, 6).

77

A PERFECT HEART

For the eyes of the LORD run to and fro throughout the whole earth, to show himself strong in the behalf of them whose heart is perfect toward him.
—2 Chronicles 16:9 KJV

In worldly matters, we know how important it is that work be done with the whole heart. In the spiritual realm, this rule still holds true. God has given the commandment, *"You shall love the LORD your God with all your heart...and with all your strength"* (Deuteronomy 6:5). In Jeremiah we read, *"You will seek Me and find Me, when you search for Me with all your heart"* (Jeremiah 29:13).

It is amazing that earnest Christians, who attend to their daily work with all their hearts, are so content to take things easy in the service of God. They do not realize that, if in anything, they should give themselves to God's service with all the power of their wills.

In the words of 2 Chronicles 16:9, we are given insight into the absolute necessity of seeking God with a perfect heart: *"The eyes of the LORD run to and fro throughout the whole earth, to show himself strong in the behalf of them whose heart is perfect toward him."*

What an encouragement this should be to us to humbly wait on God with an upright heart! We may be assured that His eye will be upon us and that He will show forth His mighty power in us and in our work.

Oh Christian, have you learned this lesson in your worship of God, yielding yourself each morning, yielding your whole heart to do God's will? Pray each prayer with a perfect heart in true wholehearted devotion to Him. Then expect, by faith, the power of God to work in you and through you.

Remember that in order to come to this, you must begin by being silent before God, until you realize that He is indeed working in secret in your heart.

I wait for my God. (Psalm 69:3)

In the secret place of His tabernacle He shall hide me. (Psalm 27:5)

78

THE OMNIPOTENCE OF GOD

I am Almighty God.
—Genesis 17:1

When Abraham heard these words, he fell on his face. God spoke to him and filled his heart with faith in what God would do for him.

Oh Christian, have you bowed in deep humility before God, until you felt that you were in living contact with the Almighty; until your heart has been filled with the faith that the almighty God is working in you and will perfect His work in you?

Read in the Psalms how believers gloried in God and in His strength: *"I will love You, O Lord, my strength"* (Psalm 18:1); *"God is the strength of my heart"* (Psalm 73:26); *"The Lord is the strength of my life"* (Psalm 27:1); *"It is God who arms me with strength"* (Psalm 18:32); *"God is our refuge and strength"* (Psalm 46:1). Take hold of these words, and take time to adore God as the Almighty One, your strength.

Christ taught us that salvation is the work of God, and quite impossible to man. When the disciples asked, *"Who then can be saved?"* (Matthew 19:25), His answer was, *"With men this is impossible, but with God all things are possible"* (v. 26). If we firmly believe this, we will have courage to believe that God is working in us all that is well pleasing in His sight.

Remember how Paul prayed for the Ephesians, that through the enlightening of the Spirit they might know *"the exceeding greatness of His power toward us who believe, according to the working of His mighty power"* (Ephesians 1:19). For the Colossians he prayed that they might be *"strengthened with all might, according to His glorious power"* (Colossians 1:11). When a person fully believes that the mighty power of God is working unceasingly within him, he can joyfully say, *"The Lord is the strength of my life"* (Psalm 27:1).

Do you wonder why many Christians complain of weakness and shortcomings? They do not understand that the almighty God must work in them every hour of the day. That is the secret of the true life of faith.

Do not rest until you can say to God, *"I will love You, O Lord, my strength"* (Psalm 18:1). Let God have complete possession of you, and you will be able to say with all God's people, *"You are the glory of their strength"* (Psalm 89:17).

THE FEAR OF GOD

Blessed is the man who fears the LORD,
who delights greatly in His commandments.
—Psalm 112:1

The fear of God—these words characterize the religion of the Old Testament and the foundation that it laid for the more abundant life of the New. The gift of holy fear is still the great desire of each child of God, and it is an essential part of a life that is to make a real impression on the world around. It is one of the great promises of the new covenant in Jeremiah: *"I will make an everlasting covenant with them…[and] I will put My fear in their hearts so that they will not depart from Me"* (Jeremiah 32:40).

We find the perfect combination of the two in Acts 9:31: *"Then the churches throughout all Judea, Galilee, and Samaria had peace and were edified. And walking in the fear of the Lord and in the comfort of the Holy Spirit, they were multiplied."* More than once, Paul gave the fear of God a high place in the Christian life: *"Work out your own salvation with fear and trembling; for it is God who works in you"* (Philippians 2:12–13); *"Perfecting holiness in the fear of God"* (2 Corinthians 7:1).

It has often been said that the lack of the fear of God is one of the things in which our modern times cannot compare favorably with the times of the Puritans. It is no wonder that there is so much cause of complaint in regard to the reading of God's Word, the worship of His house, and the absence of the spirit of continuous prayer that marked the early church. We need texts like the one at the beginning of this devotion to be expounded, and young converts must be fully instructed in the need for and the blessedness of a deep fear of God, leading to an unceasing prayerfulness as one of the essential elements of the life of faith.

Let us earnestly cultivate this grace in the inner chamber. Let us hear these words coming out of the very heavens:

> *Who shall not fear You, O Lord, and glorify Your name? For You alone are holy.* (Revelation 15:4)

> *Let us have grace, by which we may serve God acceptably with reverence and godly fear.* (Hebrews 12:28)

"Blessed is the man who fears the LORD." As we take these words into our hearts and believe that this is one of the deepest secrets of blessedness, we will seek to worship Him in holy fear.

> *Serve the LORD with fear, and rejoice with trembling.* (Psalm 2:11)

80

GOD INCOMPREHENSIBLE

Behold, God is great, and we do not know Him.
—Job 36:26

As for the Almighty, we cannot find Him;
He is excellent in power.
—Job 37:23

This attribute of God, as a Spirit whose being and glory are entirely beyond our power of comprehension, is one that we ponder all too little. And yet in the spiritual life, it is of the utmost importance to feel deeply that, as the heavens are high above the earth, so God's thoughts and ways are infinitely exalted beyond all our thoughts (Isaiah 55:9).

It is only right that we look up to God with deep humility and holy reverence, and then with childlike simplicity yield ourselves to the teaching of His Holy Spirit. *"Oh, the depth of the riches both of the wisdom and knowledge of God! How unsearchable are His judgments and His ways past finding out!"* (Romans 11:33).

Let our hearts respond, "Oh Lord, oh God of gods, how wonderful You are in all Your thoughts, and how deep in Your purposes!" The study of what God is should always fill us with holy awe, and the sacred longing to know and honor Him rightly.

Just think—

His greatness…Incomprehensible

His might…Incomprehensible

His omnipresence…Incomprehensible

His wisdom…Incomprehensible

His holiness…Incomprehensible

His mercy…Incomprehensible

His love…Incomprehensible

As we worship, let us cry out, "What an inconceivable glory is in this great Being who is my God and Father!" Confess with shame how little you have sought to know Him fully or to wait upon Him to reveal Himself. Begin in faith to trust that, in a way passing all understanding, this incomprehensible and allglorious God will work in your heart and life and allow you, in ever growing measure, to know Him fully.

My eyes are upon You, O GOD the Lord; in You I take refuge. (Psalm 141:8)

Be still, and know that I am God. (Psalm 46:10)

81

THE HOLINESS OF GOD IN THE OLD TESTAMENT

Be holy, for I am holy.
—Leviticus 11:45

I am the LORD who sanctifies you.
—Leviticus 20:8

These two ideas are recorded nine times in Leviticus. (See Leviticus 19:2; 20:7; 21:8, 15, 23; 22:9, 16.) Israel had to learn that, just as holiness is the highest and most glorious attribute of God, so it must be the obvious characteristic of His people. He who desires to know God fully and to meet Him in secret must above all desire to be holy as He is holy.

The priests who were to have access to God had to be set apart for a life of holiness. It was the same for the prophet Isaiah who was to speak for Him: *"I saw the Lord sitting on a throne, high and lifted up....[And the seraphim] said: 'Holy holy, holy is the LORD of hosts'"* (Isaiah 6:1, 3). This is the voice of adoration.

"So I said: 'Woe is me, for I am undone!...For my eyes have seen the King, the LORD of hosts'" (v. 5). This is the voice of a broken, contrite heart.

Then one of the seraphim touched Isaiah's mouth with a live coal from the altar and said, *"Behold, this has touched your lips; your iniquity is taken away, and your sin purged"* (v. 7). This is the voice of grace and full redemption.

Then follows the voice of God: *"Whom shall I send?"* (v. 8). And the willing answer is, *"Here am I! Send me"* (v. 8). Pause with holy fear, and ask God to reveal Himself as the Holy One. *"For thus says the High and Lofty One who inhabits eternity, whose name is Holy: 'I dwell in the high and holy place, with him who has a contrite and humble spirit'"* (Isaiah 57:15).

Be still, and take time to worship God in His great glory and in that deep condescension in which He longs and offers to dwell with us and in us.

Child of God, if you wish to meet your Father in secret, bow low and worship Him in the glory of His holiness. Give Him time to make Himself known to you. It is indeed an unspeakable grace to know God as the Holy One.

You shall be holy, for I the LORD your God am holy.
(Leviticus 19:2)

Holy, holy, holy is the LORD of hosts.   (Isaiah 6:3)

Worship the LORD in the beauty of holiness!
(1 Chronicles 16:29)

Let the beauty of the LORD our God be upon us.
(Psalm 90:17)

82

THE HOLINESS OF GOD IN THE NEW TESTAMENT

Holy Father, keep through Your name those whom You have given Me.…Sanctify them.…And for their sakes I sanctify Myself, that they also may be sanctified by the truth.
—John 17:11, 17, 19

Christ always lives to pray this great prayer. Expect and take hold of God's answer.

Read the words of the apostle Paul in 1 Thessalonians: "*Night and day praying exceedingly…that He* [the Lord] *may establish your hearts blameless in holiness before our God*" (1 Thessalonians 3:10, 13); "*The God of peace Himself sanctify you completely…who also will do it*" (1 Thessalonians 5:23–24).

Ponder deeply these words as you read them, and use them as a prayer to God: "Blessed Lord, strengthen my heart to be '*blameless in holiness.*' Sanctify me wholly. I know that You are faithful, and You will do it."

What a privilege to commune with God in secret, to speak these words in prayer, and then to wait upon Him until, through the working of the Spirit, they live in our hearts and we begin to know something of the holiness of God!

God's holiness has been revealed in the Old Testament. In the New, we find the holiness of God's people in Christ, through the sanctification of the Spirit. Oh, that we understood the blessedness of God's saying, *"Be holy, for I am holy"* (Leviticus 11:45)!

God is saying to us, "With you, My children, as it is with Me, holiness should be the chief thing." For this purpose, the Holy One has revealed Himself to us through the Son and the Holy Spirit. Let us use the word *holy* with great reverence of God, and then, for ourselves, with holy desire. Worship the God who says, *"I am the LORD who sanctifies you"* (Leviticus 22:32).

Bow before Him in holy fear and strong desire, and then, in the fullness of faith, listen to the prayer promise: *"The God of peace Himself sanctify you completely…who also will do it"* (1 Thessalonians 5:23–24).

83

SIN

And the grace of our Lord was exceedingly abundant, with faith and love which are in Christ Jesus.…Christ Jesus came into the world to save sinners, of whom I am chief.
—1 Timothy 1:14–15

Never forget for a moment as you enter the secret chamber, that your whole relationship to God depends on what you think of sin and of yourself as a redeemed sinner.

It is sin that makes God's holiness so amazing. It is sin that makes God's holiness so glorious, because He has said: *"Be holy, for I am holy*" (Leviticus 11:45); "*I am the* LORD *who sanctifies you*" (Leviticus 22:32).

It is sin that called forth the wonderful love of God in not sparing His Son. It was sin that nailed Jesus to the cross and revealed the depth and the power of the love with which He loved. Through all eternity in the glory of heaven, it is our being redeemed sinners that will give music to our praise.

Never forget for a moment that it is sin that has led to the great transaction between you and Christ Jesus. Each day in your fellowship with God, His one aim is to deliver and keep you fully from its power, and to lift you up into His likeness and His infinite love.

It is the thought of sin that will keep you low at His feet and will give the deep undertone to all your adoration. It is the thought of sin, ever surrounding you and seeking to tempt you, that will give fervency to your prayer and urgency to the faith that hides itself in Christ. It is the thought of sin that makes Christ so unspeakably precious, that keeps you every moment dependent on His grace, and that gives you the right to be more than a conqueror "*through Him who loved us*" (Romans 8:37). It is the thought of sin that calls you to thank God with "*a broken and a contrite heart...* [that] God...will not despise*" (Psalm 51:17), and that works in you a contrite and humble spirit in which He delights to dwell.

It is in the inner chamber, in secret with the Father, that sin can be conquered, the holiness of Christ can be imparted, and the Spirit of holiness can take possession of our lives. It is in the inner chamber that we learn to know and experience fully the divine power of these precious words of promise: "*The blood of Jesus Christ His Son cleanses us from all sin*" (1 John 1:7), and "*Whoever abides in Him does not sin*" (1 John 3:6).

84

THE MERCY OF GOD

Oh, give thanks to the Lord, for He is good!
For His mercy endures forever.
—Psalm 136:1

This Psalm is wholly devoted to the praise of God's mercy. In each of the twentysix verses, we have the expression, *"His mercy endures forever."* The psalmist was full of this glad thought. Our hearts, too, should be filled with this blessed assurance. The everlasting, unchangeable mercy of God is cause for unceasing praise and thanksgiving.

Read what is said about God's mercy in the well-known Psalm 103: *"Bless the Lord, O my soul, and forget not all His benefits… who crowns you with lovingkindness and tender mercies"* (vv. 2, 4). Of all God's other attributes, mercy is the crown. May it be a crown upon my head and in my life!

"The Lord is merciful and gracious…and abounding in mercy" (v. 8). As wonderful as God's greatness is, so infinite is His mercy: *"As the heavens are high above the earth, so great is His mercy toward those who fear Him"* (v. 11). What a thought! As high as heaven is above the earth, so immeasurably and inconceivably great is the mercy of God while He waits to bestow His richest blessing.

"The mercy of the Lord is from everlasting to everlasting on those who fear Him" (v. 17). Here again the psalmist spoke of God's boundless lovingkindness and mercy.

How frequently we have read these familiar words without the least thought of their immeasurable greatness! Be still, and meditate until your heart responds in the words of Psalm 36: *"Your mercy, O LORD, is in the heavens"* (v. 5); *"How precious is Your lovingkindness, O God! Therefore the children of men put their trust under the shadow of Your wings"* (v. 7); *"Oh, continue Your lovingkindness to those who know You"* (v. 10).

Take time to thank God with great joy for the wonderful mercy with which He crowns your life, and say: *"Your lovingkindness is better than life"* (Psalm 63:3).

85

THE WORD OF GOD

The word of God is living and powerful.
—Hebrews 4:12

Both the Word of God and prayer are indispensable for communion with God, and in the inner chamber they should not be separated. In His Word, God speaks to us; in prayer, we speak to God.

The Word teaches us to know the God to whom we pray. It teaches us how He wants us to pray. It gives us precious promises to encourage us in prayer. It often gives us wonderful answers to prayer.

The Word comes from God's heart and brings His thoughts and His love into our hearts. And then, through prayer, the Word goes back from our hearts into His great heart of love. Prayer is the means of fellowship between God's heart and ours.

The Word teaches us God's will—the will of His promises as to what He will do for us, and also the will of His commands. His promises are food for our faith, and to His commands we surrender ourselves in loving obedience.

The more we pray, the more we will feel our need for the Word and will rejoice in it. The more we read God's Word, the more we will have to pray about, and the more power we will have in prayer. One great cause of prayerlessness is that we read God's Word too little, only superficially, or in the light of human wisdom.

The Holy Spirit, through whom the Word has been spoken, is also the Spirit of prayer. He will teach us how to receive the Word and how to approach God.

How blessed the inner chamber would be, what a power and an inspiration in our worship, if we only took God's Word as from Himself, turning it into prayer and definitely expecting an answer! It is in the inner chamber, in God's presence, that by the Holy Spirit God's Word will become our delight and our strength.

When we take God's Word in deepest reverence in our hearts, on our lips, and in our lives, it will be a never failing fountain of strength and blessing to us. Let us believe that God's Word is indeed full of power that will make us strong, able to expect and receive great things from God. Above all, it will give us the daily blessed fellowship with Him as the living God.

Blessed is the man [whose] *delight is in the law of the* LORD, *and in His law he meditates day and night.* (Psalm 1:1–2)

86

THE GLORY OF GOD

To Him be glory...to all generations.
—Ephesians 3:21

God Himself must reveal His glory to us; only then are we able to know and glorify Him rightly.

There is no more wonderful image of the glory of God in nature than we find in the starry heavens. Telescopes, which are continually made more powerful, have long proclaimed the wonders of God's universe. And by means of photography, the wonders of that glory have been revealed. A photographic plate fixed below the telescope will reveal millions of stars that could never have been seen by the eye through even the best telescope. Man must step aside and allow the glory of the heavens to reveal itself; and the stars, at first wholly invisible, will leave their image upon the plate.

What a lesson for the believer who longs to see the glory of God in His Word! Put aside your own efforts and thoughts. Let your heart be like a photographic plate that waits for God's glory to be revealed. As the plate must be prepared and clean, let your heart be prepared and purified by God's Spirit. *"Blessed are the pure in heart, for they shall see God"* (Matthew 5:8). As the plate must be stationary, let your heart be still before God. As the plate must be exposed up to seven or eight hours in order to obtain the full impression of the farthest stars, let your heart take time in silent waiting upon God, and He will reveal His glory.

If you are silent before God and give Him time, He will put thoughts into your heart that may be of unspeakable blessing to yourself and others. He will create within you desires and dispositions that will indeed be as the rays of His glory shining in you.

Test this principle today. Offer your spirit to God in deep humility, and have faith that He will reveal Himself in His holy love. His glory will descend upon you. You will feel the need of giving Him full time to do His blessed work.

> *My soul, wait silently for God alone, for my expectation is from Him.*   (Psalm 62:5)

> *Be still, and know that I am God.*   (Psalm 46:10)

87

THE HOLY TRINITY

Elect according to the foreknowledge of God the Father,
in sanctification of the Spirit, for obedience and sprinkling
of the blood of Jesus Christ.
—1 Peter 1:2

Here is one of the Scriptures in which we see that the great truth of the blessed Trinity lies at the very root of our spiritual lives. In this book, I have written much about the adoration of God the Father and about the need for enough time each day to worship Him in some of His glorious attributes. But we must remind ourselves that, for all our fellowship with God, the presence and power of the Son and the Spirit are absolutely necessary.

What a realm this opens for us in the inner chamber! We need time to realize how all our fellowship with the Father is determined by the active and personal presence and working of the Lord Jesus. It takes time to become fully conscious of how much we need Him every time we approach Him, of what confidence we may have in the work that He is doing for us and in us, and of what the holy and intimate love is in which we may count upon His presence and allprevailing intercession. But, oh, to learn the lesson that prayer takes time, and that that time will be most blessedly rewarded!

It is the same with the divine and almighty power of the Holy Spirit working in the depths of our hearts as the One who alone is able to reveal the Son within each of us. Through Him alone we have the power to know what and how to pray; above all, through Him we know how to plead the name of Jesus and to receive the assurance that our prayers have been accepted.

Dear reader, have you not felt more than once that it was almost a mockery to speak of spending five minutes alone with God to come under the impression of His glory? And now, does not the thought of the true worship of God in Christ through the Holy Spirit make you feel more than ever that it takes time to enter into such holy alliance with God and to keep the heart and mind in His peace and presence throughout the day? By waiting in the secret of God's presence, you receive grace to abide in Christ and to be led by His Spirit all day long.

Just pause and think: *"Elect according to the foreknowledge of God the Father, in sanctification of the Spirit, for obedience and sprinkling of the blood of Jesus Christ."* What food for thought and worship!

> *When You said, "Seek My face," my heart said to You, "Your face, LORD, I will seek."* (Psalm 27:8)

88

THE LOVE OF GOD

God is love, and he who abides in love abides in God,
and God in him.
—1 John 4:16

The best and most wonderful word in heaven is *love*, for "*God is love.*" And the best and most wonderful word in the inner chamber must also be *love*, for the God who meets us there is love.

What is love? It is the deep desire to give itself for the one who is loved. Love finds its joy in imparting all that it has in order to make the loved one happy. And the heavenly Father, who offers to meet us in the inner chamber—let there be no doubt of this in our minds—has no other aim than to fill our hearts with His love.

All the other attributes of God that have been mentioned find their highest glory in this. The true and full blessing of the inner chamber is nothing less than a life lived in the abundant love of God.

Because of this, our first and chief thought in the inner chamber should be faith in the love of God. As you set yourself to pray, seek to exercise great and unbounded faith in the love of God.

Take time in silence to meditate on the wonderful revelation of God's love in Christ, until you are filled with the spirit of worship and wonder and longing desire. Take time to believe the precious truth: *"The love of God has been poured out in our hearts by the Holy Spirit who was given to us"* (Romans 5:5).

Let us remember with shame how little we have believed in and sought this love. As we pray, let us be assured that our heavenly Father longs to manifest His love to us. We can say aloud, "I am deeply convinced of the truth. He can and will do it."

Yes, I have loved you with an everlasting love.
(Jeremiah 31:3)

That you, being rooted and grounded in love, may be able to comprehend with all the saints what is the width and length and depth and height; to know the love of Christ which passes knowledge. (Ephesians 3:17–19)

Behold what manner of love the Father has bestowed on us.
(1 John 3:1)

89

WAITING ON GOD

On You I wait all the day.
—Psalm 25:5

Waiting on God—in this expression we find one of the deepest truths of God's Word in regard to the attitude of the soul in its communion with God.

As we wait on God—just think—He will reveal Himself in us, He will teach us all His will, He will do to us what He has promised, and in all things He will be the Infinite God.

Such is the attitude with which each day should begin. In the inner chamber, in quiet meditation, in expressing our ardent desires through prayer, in the course of our daily work, in all our striving after obedience and holiness, in all our struggles against sin and self-will—in everything we must wait on God to receive what He will bestow, to see what He will do, and to allow Him to be the almighty God.

Meditate on these things, and they will help you to truly value the precious promises of God's Word. In this we have the secret of heavenly power and joy:

> *Those who wait on the LORD shall renew their strength; they shall mount up with wings like eagles.* (Isaiah 40:31)

> *Wait on the LORD; be of good courage, and He shall strengthen your heart; wait, I say, on the LORD!* (Psalm 27:14)

> *Rest in the LORD, and wait patiently for Him.* (Psalm 37:7)

The deep root of all scriptural theology is absolute dependence on God. As we exercise this attitude, it will become more natural and blessedly possible to say, *"On You I wait all the day."* Here we have the secret of true, uninterrupted, silent adoration and worship of God.

Has this book helped to teach you the true worship of God? If so, the Lord's name be praised. Or have you only learned how little you know of it? For this, too, let us thank Him.

If you desire a fuller experience of this blessing, read this book again with a deeper insight into what is meant, and a greater knowledge of the absolute need of each day and all day waiting on God. May the God of all grace grant this.

> *I wait for the LORD, my soul waits, and in His word I do hope.* (Psalm 130:5)

Rest in the Lord, *and wait patiently for Him…and He shall give you the desires of your heart.* (Psalm 37:7, 4)

90

THE PRAISE OF GOD

Praise from the upright is beautiful.
—Psalm 33:1

Praise will always be a part of adoration. Adoration, when it has entered God's presence and has fellowshipped with Him, will always lead to the praise of His name. Let praise be a part of the incense we bring before God in our quiet time.

When the children of Israel, at their birth as the people of God at the Red Sea, had been delivered from the power of Egypt, their joy of redemption burst forth in the song of Moses, filled with praise: *"Who is like You, O* Lord, *among the gods? Who is like You, glorious in holiness, fearful in praises, doing wonders?"* (Exodus 15:11).

In the Psalms we see what a large place praise ought to have in the spiritual life. There are more than sixty psalms of praise, becoming more frequent as the book draws to its close. (See Psalm 95–101, 103–107, 111–118, 134–138, 144–150.) The last five are Hallelujah psalms, with the words *"Praise the* Lord*"* at the beginning and the end. The very last psalm repeats *"Praise Him"* twice in every verse, and it ends with, *"Let everything that has breath praise the* Lord*"* (Psalm 150:6).

Take time to study this until your heart and life are entirely a continual song of praise: *"I will bless the LORD at all times; His praise shall continually be in my mouth"* (Psalm 34:1); *"Every day I will bless You"* (Psalm 145:2); *"I will sing praises to my God while I have my being"* (Psalm 146:2).

With the coming of Christ into the world, there was a new outburst of praise in the song of the angels, the song of Mary, the song of Zechariah, and the song of Simeon. And then, in *"the song of Moses...and the song of the Lamb"* (Revelation 15:3), we find the praise of God filling creation: *"Great and marvelous are Your works, Lord God Almighty!...Who shall not fear You, O Lord, and glorify Your Name? For You alone are holy"* (vv. 3–4). This song of praise ends with the fourfold *"Alleluia!"* (Revelation 19:1, 3–4, 6). *"For the Lord God Omnipotent reigns!"* (v. 6).

Oh child of God, let the inner chamber and your quiet time with God always lead your heart to unceasing praise!

91

THE LOST SECRET

Wait for the Promise of the Father....You shall be baptized with the Holy Spirit not many days from now.
—Acts 1:4–5

After our Lord had given the great command, *"Go into all the world and preach the gospel to every creature"* (Mark 16:15), He added His very last command: *"Tarry in the city of Jerusalem until you are endued with power from on high"* (Luke 24:49); *"Wait for the Promise of the Father....You shall be baptized with the Holy Spirit not many days from now."*

All Christians agree that the great command to preach the Gospel to every creature was not only for the disciples, but is our obligation as well. But not everyone appears to believe that Christ's very last command—not to preach until they had received the power from on high—is as binding on us as it was on the disciples. The church seems to have lost possession of what ought to be her secret of secrets—the daily, abiding consciousness that only as she lives in the power of the Holy Spirit can she preach the Gospel with Spirit and power. Therefore, there is much preaching and working with little spiritual result. It is owing to nothing but this that the universal complaint is heard that there is too little prayer, especially that much-availing prayer that brings down the power from on high. Without the baptism of the Holy Spirit, prayer is not likely to produce results.

I desire to study the secret of Pentecost as it is revealed in the words and deeds of our blessed Master, and in the words and deeds of His disciples as they took Him at His word and continued with one accord in prayer and supplication until the promise was fulfilled. As the disciples were filled with the Holy Spirit, they proved what the mighty power of their God could do through them.

Let us seek earnestly the grace of the Holy Spirit, who alone can reveal to us what *"eye has not seen, nor ear heard, nor have entered into the heart of man,"* that is, *"the things which God has prepared for those who love Him"* (1 Corinthians 2:9). Let us pray that the lost secret may be found—the sure promise that in answer to fervent prayer, the power of the Holy Spirit will indeed be given.

THE KINGDOM OF GOD

*[Jesus] presented Himself alive [to His disciples]...being
seen by them during forty days and speaking of the things
pertaining to the kingdom of God.*
—Acts 1:3

When Christ began to preach, He took up the message of John: *"The kingdom of heaven is at hand"* (Matthew 4:17). Later on He said, *"There are some standing here who will not taste death till they see the kingdom of God present with power"* (Mark 9:1). This could not be until the King had ascended His throne. Then He and His disciples would be ready to receive the great gift of the Holy Spirit, bringing down the kingdom of God into their hearts.

Acts 1:3 tells us that all the teaching of Jesus during the forty days after the Resurrection dealt with the kingdom of God. It is remarkable how Luke, in the last verses of Acts, summed up all the teaching of Paul at Rome, who *"testified of the kingdom of God"* (Acts 28:23) and was *"preaching the kingdom of God"* (v. 31).

Christ, seated upon the throne of God, was now King and Lord of all. To His disciples He had entrusted the announcement of the kingdom, which is *"righteousness and peace and joy in the Holy Spirit"* (Romans 14:17). The prayer He had taught them—*"Our Father in heaven...Your kingdom come"* (Luke 11:2)—now had a new meaning for them. The reign of God in heaven came down in the power of the Spirit, and the disciples were full of this one thought: to preach the coming of the Spirit into the hearts of men.

There were now on earth good tidings of the kingdom of God—a kingdom of God ruling and dwelling with men, even as in heaven.

When Jesus spoke about the kingdom of God in Acts 1, He implied all the essential characteristics of a kingdom. Thus, I will expound upon these six marks of the kingdom of God. The first two characteristics of every kingdom are the king and his subjects. We know the King of God's government to be the crucified Christ, and the disciples His faithful followers. Acts 1:8 tells us of a power that enabled the disciples to serve their King, and that was the Holy Spirit, the third mark of a kingdom. Their work was to testify of Christ as His witnesses, and their aim was to reach the ends of the earth—the fourth and fifth marks of a kingdom. But before they could begin, their first duty was to wait on God in united, unceasing prayer, and so we have the sixth mark of a kingdom.

If we are to take up and continue the prayer of the disciples, it is essential to have a clear and full impression of all that Christ spoke to them in that last moment, and what it meant for their inner lives and all their service.

93

CHRIST AS KING

And He said to them, "Assuredly, I say to you that there are some standing here who will not taste death till they see the kingdom of God present with power."
—Mark 9:1

The first mark of the kingdom of God, the church, is that Christ is King. Christ and John had both preached that the kingdom of God was *"at hand"* (Matthew 3:2; 4:17). In Mark 9:1 Christ said that the kingdom would come in power during the lifetimes of some who heard Him. That could mean nothing else but that when He, as King, had ascended the throne of the Father, the kingdom would be revealed in the hearts of His disciples by the power of the Holy Spirit. In the kingdom of heaven, God's will was always being done; in the power of the Holy Spirit, Christ's disciples would do His will on earth as it was done in heaven.

The characteristics of a kingdom can be seen in its king. Christ now reigns on the throne of the Father. There is no external manifestation of the kingdom on earth; rather, its power is seen in the lives of those in whom it rules. It is only in the church, the members of Christ, that the united body can be seen and known. Christ lives and dwells and rules in their hearts. Our Lord Himself taught how close the relationship would be: *"At that day you will know that I am in My Father, and you in Me, and I in you"* (John 14:20). The faith of His oneness with God and His omnipotent power would be next to the knowledge that they lived in Him and He in them.

This must be our first lesson if we are to follow in the steps of the disciples and share their blessing. We must know that Christ, as King, dwells and rules in our hearts. We must know that we live in Him and by His power are able to accomplish all that He wants us to do. Our lives are to be entirely devoted to our King and the service of His kingdom.

This blessed relationship to Christ means, above all, a daily fellowship with Him in prayer. The prayer life is to be a continuous and unbroken exercise. It is in this way that His people can rejoice in their King and can be *"more than conquerors"* (Romans 8:37) in Him.

THE CRUCIFIED JESUS

God has made this Jesus, whom you crucified,
both Lord and Christ.
—Acts 2:36

The King of the kingdom of heaven is none other than the crucified Jesus. All that we have to say of Him, of His divine power, His abiding presence, and His wonderful love, does not teach us to know Him fully unless we maintain the deep awareness that our King is the crucified Jesus. God has placed Him *"in the midst of [His] throne"* as a Lamb, *"as though it had been slain"* (Revelation 5:6), and it is thus that the hosts of heaven adore Him. It is thus that we worship Him as a King.

Christ's cross is His highest glory. It is through this that He has conquered every enemy and gained His place on the throne of God. And it is this that He will impart to us, too, if we are to know fully the meaning of victory over sin. When Paul wrote, *"I have been crucified with Christ…Christ lives in me"* (Galatians 2:20), he taught us that Christ ruled on the throne of his heart as the Crucified One, and that the spirit of the cross would triumph over us as it did in Him.

This was true of the disciples. This was their deepest preparation for receiving the Holy Spirit. With their Lord, they had been crucified to the world. The *"old man"* (Romans 6:6) had been crucified; in Him they were *"dead indeed to sin"* (v. 11), and their lives were *"hidden with Christ in God"* (Colossians 3:3). Each one of us needs to experience this fellowship with Christ in His cross if the Spirit of Pentecost is really to take possession of us. It was through the eternal Spirit that Christ gave Himself as a sacrifice and became the King on the throne of God. As we become *"conformed to His death"* (Philippians 3:10) in the entire surrender of our wills, and in the entire selfdenial of our old natures, in the entire separation from the spirit of this world, we can become the worthy servants of a crucified King, and our hearts the worthy temples of His glory.

95

THE APOSTLES

Being assembled together with them, he charged them
not to depart from Jerusalem, but to wait for
the promise of the Father.
—Acts 1:4 RV

The second mark of the church is found in the disciples whom the Lord had prepared to receive His Spirit and to be His witnesses. If we want to understand fully the outpouring of the Spirit in answer to the prayer of the disciples, we must above all ask, "What was in these men that enabled them to speak forth such powerful, effective prayer, and to receive the wonderful fulfillment of the promise that came to them?" They were simple, uneducated men with many faults whom the Lord had called to forsake all and follow Him. They had done this as far as they could; they followed Him in the life He led and the work He did. Though there was much sin in them and they had as yet no power to deny themselves fully, their hearts clung to Him in deep sincerity. In the midst of much stumbling, they followed Him to the cross. They shared with Him His death; unconsciously, but in truth, they died with Him to sin and were raised with Him in the power of a new life. It was this that prepared them for power in prayer and for being clothed with the *"power from on high"* (Luke 24:49).

Let this be the test by which we examine ourselves: have we indeed surrendered to the fellowship of Christ's sufferings and death? Have we hated our own lives and crucified them? And have we received the power of Christ's life in us? It is this that will give us liberty to believe that God will hear our prayers. It is this that will assure us that God will give us His Holy Spirit to work in us what we and He desire. Let us indeed with one accord take up the disciples' prayer and share in the answer. We must, like them, be willing learners in the school of Jesus, and we must seek, above everything, the intimate fellowship with Him that will prepare us for praying the prayer of Pentecost and receiving its answer.

96

NOT OF THIS WORLD

They are not of the world, just as I am not of the world.
—John 17:14

During His last night, our Lord took great effort to make clear to His disciples the impassable gulf between Him and the world, and between them and the world. He had said of the Spirit, *"The world cannot receive* [Him], *because it neither sees Him nor knows Him"* (John 14:17). *"Because you are not of the world...therefore the world hates you"* (John 15:19).

One great characteristic of the disciples was that they were to be as separated from the world as Christ had been. They and Christ had become united in the Cross and the Resurrection; they both belonged to another world, the kingdom of heaven. This separation from the world is to be the mark of all believers who long to be filled with the Spirit.

Why is faith in the Holy Spirit so seldom preached and practiced in Christendom? The world rules too much in the lives of Christians. Christians rarely live the heavenly life to which they are called in Christ Jesus. The love of the world, *"the lust of the flesh, the lust of the eyes, and the pride of life"* (1 John 2:16)—that is to say, pleasure in eating, drinking, ease, and comfort; delight in all that the world offers of beauty and possession; and the self-exaltation in what the wisdom and power of man has accomplished—robs the heart of its desire for the true selfdenial that enables a man to receive the Holy Spirit.

If you wish to pray the Pentecostal prayer for the power of the Holy Spirit, examine yourself. Is the spirit of the world the reason that you do not love to pray the prayer that is absolutely necessary to receive the promise of the Father? May the Lord write this thought deep in every heart: the world cannot receive the Holy Spirit!

"[You] *are not of the world, just as I am not of the world."*

97

OBEDIENCE

*If you love Me, keep My commandments. And I will pray
the Father, and He will give you another Helper.*
—John 14:15–16

We have learned to know the disciples in their preparation
for the baptism of the Spirit, and we have seen what was needed
for their continuing *"with one accord"* (Acts 1:14) in prayer for the
power of the Spirit. Christ was everything to them. Even before
the Cross, He was literally their life, their one thought, their only
desire. But He was much more so after the Cross, and with the
Resurrection.

Was such devotion to Christ something particular to the disciples, not to be expected of everyone? Or was it indeed something
that the Lord asked from all who desired to be filled with the
Spirit? God expects it of all His children. The Lord needs such
individuals now, as much as He did then, to receive His Spirit and
His power, to show them forth here on earth, and, as intercessors,
to link the world to the throne of God.

Is Christ something, nothing, or everything to us? For the
unconverted, Christ is nothing. For the half-converted, the average
Christian, Christ is something. But for the true Christian, Christ
is everything. Each one who prays for the power of the Spirit must
be ready to say, "Today I yield myself with my whole heart to the
leading of the Spirit." A full surrender is the question of life or
death, an absolute necessity.

My brother or sister in Christ, you have read the words of John 14:15: *"If you love Me, keep My commandments."* The surrender to live every day, all day long, abiding in Christ and keeping His commandments, is to be the one sign of your discipleship. Only when the heart longs in everything to do God's will can the Father's love and Spirit rest upon the child of God. This was the disposition in which the disciples continued with one accord in prayer, and this will be the secret of power in our intercession as we plead for the church and the world.

98

THE HOLY SPIRIT

You shall be baptized with the Holy Spirit.... You shall
receive power when the Holy Spirit has come upon you.
—Acts 1:5, 8

The third mark of the church is the power for service through the Holy Spirit. Since the time of Adam's fall, when he lost the spirit that God had breathed into him, God's Spirit had striven with men and had worked in some with power, but He had never been able to find His permanent home in them. Only when Christ had come, had broken the power of sin by His death, and had won in the Resurrection a new life for men to live in Himself, could the Spirit of God come and take possession of the whole heart and make it a dwelling place for Christ and for God.

Nothing less than this is the power in us by which sin can be overcome and the prisoners be set free. This power is the Holy Spirit. In the Old Testament He was called *"the Spirit of God"* (Genesis 1:2). But now that the holiness of God had been magnified in the cross of Christ, and now that Christ has sanctified us so that we might be like Him, the Spirit of God's holiness descends to dwell in men and take possession of them as God's holy temple.

He is also the Spirit of the Son. On earth He led the Son first into the desert to be tempted by Satan, then to the synagogue in Nazareth to proclaim Himself as the fulfillment of what the prophet had spoken in Isaiah 61:1. (See Luke 4:18.) And so on the cross, Christ yielded Himself implicitly to the leading of the Spirit.

The Spirit now reveals Christ in us as our Life, our Strength for a perfect obedience, and the Word that is preached in the power of God.

Amazing mystery—the Spirit of God, our Life; the Spirit of Christ, our Light and Strength! As we become men and women who are led by this Spirit of the first disciples, we will have the power to pray *"the effective, fervent prayer of a righteous man [that] avails much"* (James 5:16).

99

THE POWER FROM ON HIGH

Tarry in the city of Jerusalem until you are endued
with power from on high.
—Luke 24:49

The Lord had said to the disciples, *"Without Me you can do nothing"* (John 15:5). Why, then, did He choose these powerless, helpless men to go out to conquer the world for Him? So that in their feebleness they might yield themselves and give Him, as Lord on His throne, the opportunity to show His power working through them. As the Father had done all the work in Christ when He was on earth, so Christ in heaven would now be the Great Worker, proving in them that all power had been given to Him *"in heaven and on earth"* (Matthew 28:18). Their place would be to pray, to believe, and to yield themselves to the mighty power of Christ.

The Holy Spirit would not live in them as a power of which they could have possession. But He would possess them, and their work would indeed be the work of the almighty Christ. Their whole attitude each day would be that of unceasing dependence and prayer, and of confident expectation.

The apostles had learned to know Christ intimately. They had seen all His mighty works; they had received His teaching; they had gone with Him through all His sufferings, even to His death on the cross. They had not only seen Him, but they had also known Him in the power of His resurrection and the experience of that resurrection life in their own hearts. Yet they were not capable of fully making Him known, until He Himself, from the throne of heaven, had taken possession of them by His Spirit dwelling in them.

Every minister of the Gospel is called to rest content with nothing less than the indwelling life and power of the Holy Spirit. This is to be his only preparation for preaching the Gospel in power. Nothing less than having Christ speaking through us in the power of His omnipotence will make us able ministers of the New Testament, bringing salvation to all who hear us.

MY WITNESSES

You shall be [My] witnesses.
—Acts 1:8

The fourth mark of Christ's church is that His servants are to be witnesses for Him, continually testifying of His wonderful love, His power to redeem, His continual abiding presence, and His wonderful power to work in them.

This is the only weapon that the King allows His redeemed ones to use. Without claiming authority or power, without wisdom or eloquence, without influence or position, each one is called, not only by his words, but also by his life and actions, to be a living proof and witness of what Jesus can do.

This is the only weapon they are to use in conquering men and bringing them to the feet of Christ. This is what the first disciples did. When they were filled with the Spirit, they began to speak of the mighty things that Christ had done.

It was in this power that those who were scattered abroad by persecution went forth, even as far as Antioch, preaching in the name of Jesus, so that a multitude of the unsaved believed. They had no commission from the apostles; they had no special gifts or training, but out of the fullness of their hearts they spoke of Jesus Christ. They could not be silent; they were filled with the life and love of Christ and could not help but witness for Him. It was this that gave the Gospel its power to increase; every new convert became a witness for Christ.

One non-Christian writer wrote, in regard to the persecutions, that if the Christians had only been content to keep the worship of Jesus to themselves, they would not have had to suffer. But in their zeal, they had wanted Christ to rule over all.

This is the secret of a flourishing church: every believer a witness for Jesus. And here we see that the cause of the weakness of the church is that so few are willing in daily life to testify that Jesus is Lord.

What a call to prayer! Lord, teach Your disciples the blessedness of knowing Jesus and the power of His love in such a way that they may find their highest joy in testifying of what He is and has done for them.

101

THE GOSPEL MINISTRY

You shall be witnesses to Me.
—Acts 1:8

The Spirit of truth…will testify of Me. And you also will bear witness, because you have been with Me from the beginning.
—John 15:26–27

When Christ said, "*You shall be witnesses to Me,*" He not only referred to all believers, but especially to all ministers of the Gospel. This is the high calling and the only power of the preacher of the Gospel—in everything to be a witness for Jesus.

This gives us two great truths. The first is that the preacher must place the preaching of Christ Himself above everything he teaches from the Word of God. This is what the first disciples did: *"In every house, they did not cease teaching and preaching Jesus as the Christ"* (Acts 5:42). This was what Philip did at Samaria: he *"preached Christ to them"* (Acts 8:5). And so Paul wrote, *"For I determined not to know anything among you except Jesus Christ and Him crucified"* (1 Corinthians 2:2).

The minister of the Gospel must never forget that it is especially for this that he has been set apart: to be, along with the Holy Spirit, a witness for Christ. As he does this, sinners will find salvation, and God's children will be sanctified and equipped for His service. Only in this way can Christ have His place in the hearts of His people and in the world around.

But there is a second thought of equal importance. And that is that the preacher's teaching must always be a personal testimony from his own experience of what Christ is and can do. As this note is sounded, the Holy Spirit carries the message as a living reality to the listeners' hearts. This is what will build up believers so that they can walk in such fellowship with Jesus Christ that He can reveal Himself through them. And this is what will lead them to the knowledge of the indispensable secret of spiritual health—the prayer life in daily fellowship, in childlike love, and true consecration with the Father and the Son.

Such thoughts will bring much unity in prayer and will cultivate among believers and ministers the joy of the Holy Spirit, in which the mouth speaks out of the abundance of the heart (see Matthew 12:34), to the praise and glory of our ever blessed Redeemer, Jesus Christ our Lord.

THE WHOLE WORLD

You shall be witnesses to Me...to the end of the earth.
—Acts 1:8

Here we have the fifth mark of Christ's church: reaching the whole world. These must have seemed remarkable words from the Man who, in what appeared to be absolute powerlessness, had been crucified by His enemies. How could He speak of the ends of the earth as His dominion? How could it have entered the mind of any writer to venture the prophecy that a Jew who had been crucified, whose whole life had seemingly been proved by that cross to be an utter failure and whose disciples had utterly forsaken Him in the end—that He would conquer the world by them?

But what foolishness it is on the part of those who speak of Christ as being nothing but a man! No human mind could have formed such an idea. It is the thought of God; He alone could plan and execute such a purpose.

The words that Jesus spoke to His disciples, *You shall receive power when the Holy Spirit has come upon you* (Acts 1:8), gave them the assurance that the Holy Spirit would maintain Christ's divine power in them. As Christ did His works only because the Father worked in Him, so Christ assured His disciples that He Himself from the throne of heaven would work all their works in them. They might ask what they desired and it would be done for them (John 15:7). In the strength of that promise, the church of Christ can make the ends of the earth its one aim.

Oh, that Christian people might understand that the extension of God's kingdom can only be brought about by the united, continued prayer of men and women who give their hearts wholly to wait on Christ in the assurance that what they desire He will do for them!

Oh, that God would grant that His children prove their faith in Christ by making His aim their aim, and by yielding themselves to be His witnesses in united, persevering prayer, waiting upon Him in the full assurance that He will most surely and most gloriously give all that they can ask.

My reader, become one of those intercessors who really believe that in answer to their prayers the crucified Jesus will do far more than they can ask or think (Ephesians 3:20).

103

THE WHOLE EARTH FILLED WITH HIS GLORY

Blessed be His glorious name forever! And let the whole earth be filled with His glory. Amen and Amen.
—Psalm 72:19

What a prospect—this earth, now under the power of the Evil One, renewed and filled with the glory of God's new earth in which righteousness will dwell! Though we believe it so little, it will surely come to pass; God's Word is the pledge of it. God's Son by His blood and death conquered the power of sin, and through the eternal Spirit the power of God is working out His purpose. What a vision—the whole earth *"filled with His glory"*!

But what a great and difficult work. It is nearly two thousand years since Christ gave the promise and ascended the throne, and yet more than half of the human race have never learned to know even the name of Jesus. And in the other half, millions are called by His name yet do not know Him. This great work of bringing the knowledge of Christ to every creature has been entrusted to a church that hardly thinks of her responsibility and of what the consequence of her neglect will be. We may indeed ask, "Will the work ever be done?" Blessed be His name, His power and His faithfulness are pledges that one day we will see it—the whole earth filled with the glory of God.

What a wonderful prayer our text contains: *"Let the whole earth be filled with His glory. Amen and Amen!"* It is to this prayer that every believer is called, and he can depend on the Holy Spirit to inspire and strengthen him. It is to this prayer that we desire to strengthen each other, so that every day of our lives, with all the power there is in us, we desire with one accord to pray continually in the faith of the name of Jesus and the power of His Spirit.

What blessedness to know that true prayer will indeed help and be answered! What blessedness every day of our lives to seek God's face, and with confidence to lay hold of Him and give Him no rest until the earth is full of His glory! Once again, what blessedness to unite with all God's willing children who are seeking to prepare the way for our King in this the day of His power!

THE FIRST PRAYER MEETING

These all continued with one accord in prayer
and supplication, with the women.
—Acts 1:14

The sixth mark of the early church is that they waited on the promise of the Father in united prayer. It is difficult to form a correct idea of the unspeakable importance of this first prayer meeting in the history of the kingdom—a prayer meeting that was the simple fulfillment of the command of Christ. It was to be for all time the indication of the one condition on which His presence and Spirit would be known in power. In it we have the secret key that opens the storehouse of heaven with all its blessings.

Christ had prayed that the disciples might be one, just as He and the Father were one (John 17:22). He prayed *"that they may be made perfect in one, and that the world may know that You have sent Me, and have loved them as You have loved Me"* (v. 23). We see, in the strife that was among them at the Lord's Table as to who would be chief, how far the disciples were from such a state when Christ prayed the prayer. It was only after the Resurrection and after Christ had gone to heaven that they were brought, in the ten days of united supplication, to that holy unity of love and purpose that would make them the one body of Christ prepared to receive the Spirit in all His power.

What a prayer meeting! It was the fruit of Christ's training during His three years of fellowship with them. Adam's body was created before God breathed His Spirit into him; likewise, the body of Christ had to be formed before the Spirit could take possession.

This prayer meeting gave us the law of the kingdom for all time. Where Christ's disciples are linked to each other in love and yield themselves wholly to Him in undivided consecration, the Spirit will be given from heaven as the seal of God's approval, and Christ will show His mighty power. One of the great marks of the new dispensation is the united, unceasing prayer that *"avails much"* (James 5:16) and is crowned with the power of the Holy Spirit. Do we not have here the reason why, if our prayers are confined in great measure to our own church or interests, the answer cannot come in such power as we expected?

105

THE UNITY OF THE SPIRIT

Endeavoring to keep the unity of the Spirit....
There is one body and one Spirit.
—Ephesians 4:3–4

From Paul we learn how the Christian communities in different places ought to remember each other in the fellowship of prayer. He pointed out how God is glorified in such prayer. So he wrote more than once about how the ministry of intercession abounds to the glory of God. (See 2 Corinthians 1:11; 4:15; 9:12–13.)

In today's church, there is a great need for the children of God throughout the world to be drawn close together in the knowledge of having been chosen by God to be a holy priesthood (see 1 Peter 2:9), ministering continually the *"sacrifice of praise"* (Jeremiah 33:11) and prayer. There is too little distinction between the world and the body of Christ; in the lives of many of God's children there is very little difference from what the world is. It is a question of the deepest importance: What can be done to foster the unity of the Spirit?

Nothing will help so much as the separation to a life of more prayer, interceding that God's people may prove their unity in a life of holiness and love. That will be a living testimony to the world of what it means to live for God. When Paul wrote, *"Praying always with all prayer and supplication in the Spirit, being watchful to this end with all perseverance and supplication for all the saints"* (Ephesians 6:18), he named one of the essential differences between God's people and the world.

You say you desire to bear this mark of the children of God, and to be able to pray for them so that you may prove to yourself and to others that you are indeed not of the world. Resolve in your life to carry about with you this one great distinctive feature of the true Christian—a life of prayer and intercession. Join with God's children who are unceasingly seeking God with one accord to maintain the *"unity of the Spirit"* and the body of Christ, to *"be strong in the Lord and in the power of His might"* (Ephesians 6:10), and to pray down a blessing upon His church. Let none of us think it too much to give fifteen minutes every day for meditation on some word of God connected with His promises to His church, and then to plead with Him for its fulfillment. Slowly yet surely, you will taste the blessedness of being one, heart and soul, with God's people, and you will receive the power to pray *"the effective, fervent prayer... [that] avails much"* (James 5:16).

PRAYER IN THE NAME OF CHRIST

Whatever you ask in My name, that I will do,
that the Father may be glorified in the Son.
—John 14:13

How wonderful is the link between our prayers and Christ's glorifying the Father in heaven! Much prayer on earth brings Him much glory in heaven. What an incentive to pray much, to intercede incessantly! Our prayer is indispensable to the glorifying of the Father.

During His last night on earth, Christ's desire was so deep for His disciples to learn to believe in the power of His name, and to take hold of His promise of a sure and abundant answer, that we find the promise repeated seven times. He knew how slow men are to believe in the wonderful promise of answer to prayer in His name. He desires to rouse a large and confident faith, to free our prayers from every shadow of doubt, and to teach us to look upon intercession as the most certain and most blessed way of bringing glory to God, joy to our own souls, and blessing to the perishing world around us.

If the thought comes to us that such prayer is not easy to attain, we only need to remember what Christ told His disciples. It was when the Holy Spirit came that they would have power to pray in power. In order to draw us on to yield ourselves fully to the control of the blessed Spirit, He holds out to us the precious promise: *"Ask, and you will receive, that your joy may be full"* (John 16:24).

As we believe in the power of the Spirit working in us in full measure, intercession will become to us the joy and the strength of all our service.

When Paul wrote, *"And whatever you do in word or deed, do all in the name of the Lord Jesus"* (Colossians 3:17), he reminded us how, in daily life, everything is to bear the signature of the name of Jesus. As we learn to do this, we will have the confidence to say to the Father, "As we live in Your name before men, we come to You with the full confidence that our prayers in Your name will be answered." Our lives lived among men are to be lived in communion with God. When the name of Jesus rules everything in our lives, it will give power to our prayers, too.

107

OUR HEAVENLY FATHER

Our Father in heaven.
—Luke 11:2

How simple, how beautiful, is this invocation that Christ puts on our lips! And yet how inconceivably rich is its meaning, in the fullness of the love and blessing it contains!

Just think of the book that could be written of all the memories that there have been on earth of wise and loving fathers. Just think of what this world owes to the fathers who have made their children strong and happy to give their lives for the welfare of their fellowmen. Then think how all this is only a shadow of exquisite beauty, and only a shadow of what the Father in heaven is to His children on earth.

Christ bestowed a great gift on us when He gave us the right to say "Father" to the God of the universe. We have the privilege of calling upon Him as "The Father of Christ," "Our Father," and "My Father."

We call Him *our Father in heaven,* our heavenly Father. We consider it a great privilege as we bow in worship to know that the Father comes near to us where we are upon earth. But we soon begin to feel the need to rise up to enter into His holy presence in heaven, to breathe its atmosphere, to drink in its spirit, and to become truly heavenly minded. And as our thoughts leave earth behind, and in the power of the Holy Spirit we enter the Holiest of All, where the seraphim worship, the words *heavenly Father* take on a new meaning, and our hearts come under an influence that can abide all day long.

As we then gather up our thoughts of what fatherhood on earth has meant, and as we hear the voice of Christ saying, *"How much more"* (Luke 11:13), we feel the distance between the earthly picture and the heavenly reality. And we can only bow in lowly, loving adoration, saying, "Father, our Father, my Father." Only in this way can full joy and power come to us as we rest rejoicingly in this Scripture: *"How much more will your heavenly Father give the Holy Spirit to those who ask Him!"* (v. 13).

Oh, for grace to cultivate a heavenly spirit, to prove daily that we are children who have a Father in heaven and who love to dwell in His holy presence every day!

108

THE POWER OF PRAYER

The effective, fervent prayer of a righteous man avails much.
—James 5:16

Prayer *"avails much."* It *"avails much"* with God. It *"avails much"* in the history of His church and people. Prayer is the one great power that the church can exercise in securing the working of God's omnipotence in the world.

The *"prayer of a righteous man avails much."* That is, a man who has the righteousness of Christ, not only as a garment covering him, but also as a lifepower inspiring him, is a *"new man which was created…in true righteousness and holiness"* (Ephesians 4:24), a man who lives *"as [a slave] of righteousness"* (Romans 6:19). These are the righteous whom the Lord loves and whose prayers have power. (See Psalm 66:18–19; 1 John 3:22.)

When Christ gave His great prayer promises during His last night, it was to those who keep His commandments: *"If you love Me, keep My commandments. And I will pray the Father, and He will give you another Helper"* (John 14:15–16); *"If you keep My commandments, you will abide in My love…[and] you will ask what you desire, and it shall be done for you"* (John 15:10, 7).

"The effective, fervent prayer of a righteous man avails much." It is only when the righteous man stirs up himself and rouses his whole being to take hold of God that the prayer *"avails much."* As Jacob said, *"I will not let You go"* (Genesis 32:26); as the importunate

widow gave the just judge no rest, so does the *"effective, fervent prayer"* bring about great things.

And then comes the *"effective, fervent prayer"* of many righteous people. When two or three agree, there is the promise of an answer (Matthew 18:19). How much more when hundreds and thousands unite with one accord to cry to God to display His mighty power on behalf of His people!

Let us join those who have united themselves to call upon God for the mighty power of His Holy Spirit in His church. What a great and blessed work, and what a sure prospect, in God's time, of an abundant answer! Let us ask God individually and unitedly for the grace of the *"effective, fervent prayer* [that] *avails much."*

109

PRAYER AND SACRIFICE

I want you to know what a great conflict I have for you.
—Colossians 2:1

Just as men who are undertaking a great thing in the world have to prepare themselves and use all their natural abilities to succeed, so Christians need to prepare themselves to pray with their whole hearts and strength. This is the law of the kingdom. Prayer requires the Christian to sacrifice his ease, his time, and his self. The secret of powerful prayer is sacrifice. It was the same with Christ Jesus, the Great Intercessor. It is written of Him, *"When You make His soul an offering for sin, He shall see His seed….He shall see the labor* of His soul....He shall divide the spoil with the strong, because He poured out His soul unto death" (Isaiah 53:10–12). In Gethsemane, "He had offered up prayers and supplications, with vehement cries and tears" (Hebrews 5:7). Prayer is sacrifice. The psalmist said, "Let my prayer be set before You as incense, the lifting up of my hands as the evening sacrifice" (Psalm 141:2).

Prayer is sacrifice. Our prayers have worth only from being rooted in the sacrifice of Jesus Christ. Just as He gave up everything in His prayer, "Your will be done" (Matthew 6:10), so our posture and disposition must ever be the offering up of everything to God and His service.

A pious miner had a relative whom the doctor ordered to go to a nearby state in order to get well. But there was no money. The miner resolved to take the little money that he had and ventured to use it all. He procured a comfortable lodging at a few dollars per day for the invalid. He was content with a small shack for himself and lived on only a few pennies a day for an entire month. He spent much time in prayer until he got the assurance that the invalid would recover. On the last day of the month, the sick one was well. When the miner reached home, he said that he had now learned more than ever that the secret law and hidden power of prayer lay in selfsacrifice.

Do we need to ask why we lack power in our prayers when there is so much reluctance to make the necessary sacrifice in waiting upon God? Christ, the Christ we trust in, the Christ who lives in us, offered Himself as a sacrifice to God. As this attitude lives and rules in us, we will receive power from Him as intercessors to pray the "effective, fervent prayer [that] avails much" (James 5:16).

110

THE INTERCESSION OF
THE SPIRIT FOR BELIEVERS

*He who searches the hearts knows what the mind of the
Spirit is, because He makes intercession for the saints
according to the will of God.*
—Romans 8:27

What a light these words cast upon the prayer life in the hearts of the saints! *"For we do not know what we should pray for as we ought"* (v. 26). How often this hinders our prayer or hinders the faith that is essential to its success! But here we are told for our encouragement that the Holy Spirit *"makes intercession for us with groanings which cannot be uttered"* (v. 26). *"He makes intercession for the saints according to the will of God."*

What a prospect is opened up to us here! Where and how does the Spirit make intercession for all believers? In the heart that does not know what to pray, He secretly and effectively prays what is according to the will of God. This of course implies that we trust Him to do His work in us, and that we wait before God even when we know what to pray, in the assurance that the Holy Spirit is praying in us. This further implies that we take time to wait in God's presence, that we exercise an unbounded dependence on the Holy Spirit who has been given to cry *"Abba Father"* (v. 15) within us, even when we have nothing to offer but *"groanings which cannot be uttered."*

What a difference it would make in the lives of many of God's children if they realized this! They have not only Jesus the Son of God, the great High Priest, *"always liv*[ing] *to make intercession for them"* (Hebrews 7:25); they have not only the liberty of asking in faith what they desire, and the promise that it will be given them; but they have actually the Holy Spirit, *"the Spirit of grace and supplication"* (Zechariah 12:10), to carry on, in the depths of their beings, His work of interceding for them according to the will of God.

What a call to separate ourselves from the world, to yield ourselves wholeheartedly to the leading and praying of the Spirit within us, deeper than all our thoughts or expectations! What a call to surrender ourselves in stillness of soul, resting in the Lord and waiting patiently for Him, as the Holy Spirit prays within us not only for ourselves, but especially for all believers according to the will of God!

111

THAT THEY MAY BE ONE

Holy Father, keep through Your name those whom You have given Me, that they may be one as We are....I do not pray for these alone, but also for those who will believe in Me through their word; that they all may be one, as You, Father, are in Me, and I in You; that they also may be one in Us.... And the glory which You gave Me I have given them, that they may be one just as We are one: I in them, and You in Me; that they may be made perfect in one, and that the world may know that You have sent Me.
—John 17:11, 20–23

Notice carefully how the Lord used the expression, *"that they may be one,"* five times. It is as if He felt the need of strongly placing the emphasis on these words if we are going to realize the chief thought of His high-priestly prayer. He desires that the words and the thought will indeed have the same place in our hearts that they have in His.

As He was on the way to go to the Father through the cross, He wanted us to understand that He took the thought and the desire with Him to heaven, to make it the object of His unceasing intercession there. And He entrusted the words to us, so that we would take them into the world with us and make them the object of our unceasing intercession, too. This alone would enable us to fulfill the new commandment to love our fellowmen as He loves us, so that our joy might be full (John 15:11–12).

How little the church has understood this! How little its different branches are marked by a fervent, affectionate love toward all believers of whatever name or denomination. Will we not heartily welcome the invitation to make this prayer, *"That they may be one,"* a chief part of our daily fellowship with God? How simple it would be once we connected the words *our Father* with all the children of God throughout the world. Each time we used these sacred words, we would only have to expand the little word *our* into all the largeness and riches of God's fatherly love, and our hearts would soon learn to say "our" with a childlike affection for all the saints of God, whoever and wherever they may be. We would do this as naturally as we say "Father" with the thought of His infinite love and our love for Him. The prayer *"that they may be one"* would then become a joy and a strength, a deeper bond of fellowship with Christ Jesus and all His saints, and an offer of a sweet savor to the Father of love.

112

THE DISCIPLES' PRAYER

These all continued with one accord in prayer and supplication.
—Acts 1:14

And they continued steadfastly in…fellowship…
and in prayers.
—Acts 2:42

What a lesson it would be to us in the school of prayer to have a clear understanding of what this continuing *"with one accord in prayer"* meant to the disciples!

Just think of the object of their desire. However defective the thoughts were that they had of the Blessed Spirit, this they knew from the words of Jesus: *"It is to your advantage that I go away"* (John 16:7), so that the Spirit would give the glorified Christ into their very hearts in a way they had never known Him before. And it would be He Himself, in the mighty power of God's Spirit, who would be their strength for the work to which He had called them.

With what confidence they expected the fulfillment of the promise! Had not the Master, who had loved them so well, given them the assurance of what He would send to them from the throne of the Father in heaven?

And with what intensity and persistency they pleaded! In the midst of the praise and thanksgiving that filled their hearts as they worshipped their Lord in heaven, remembering all He had taught them about importunity, they had the full assurance that He would fulfill their desires, however long the answer might be delayed. Let us nourish our hearts with thoughts such as these, until we see that the very same promise that was given to the disciples is given to us, and that we, too, even though we have to cry day and night to God, can count upon the Father to answer our prayers.

Lastly—and this is not the least—let us believe that as they continued *"with one accord in prayer,"* we also may unite in presenting our petitions even though we cannot be together in one place. In the love with which His Spirit makes us one, and in the experience of our Lord's presence with each one who joins with his fellow believers in pleading the blessed name, we can claim the promise that we, too, will be filled with the Holy Spirit.

113

PAUL'S CALL TO PRAYER

With all prayer and supplication praying at all seasons in the Spirit, and watching thereunto in all perseverance and supplication for all the saints, and on my behalf.
—Ephesians 6:18–19 RV

Paul had a deep sense of the divine unity of the whole body of Christ and of the need for unceasing prayer for all the members of the body by all who belong to it. It is evident from the words he used that he did not mean this to be an occasional thing, but the unceasing exercise of the life union in which they were bound together. *"With all prayer and supplication praying at all seasons in the Spirit, and watching thereunto in all perseverance and supplication for all the saints."*

Paul expected believers to be so filled with the consciousness of living in Christ, and through Him being united so consciously to the whole body, that in their daily lives and activities, their highest aim would always be the welfare of the body of Christ of which they had become members. He counted on their being filled with the Spirit, so that it would be perfectly natural to them—not ever a burden or constraint to them—to pray for all who belong to the body of Jesus Christ. As natural as it is for each member of my body to be ready every moment to do what is necessary for the welfare of the whole, even so, where the Holy Spirit has entire possession, the consciousness of union with Christ will always be accompanied by consciousness of the union, joy, and love of all the members.

Is this not what we need in our daily lives, that every believer who has yielded himself undividedly to Christ Jesus will daily and continually live in the consciousness that he is one with Christ and His body? Just as a war will bring to light the intensity and the readiness with which millions of the subjects of the king sacrifice their all for the king and his service, so the saints of God will live for Christ their King, and also for all the members of the body of which He is the Head. May God's people be willing for this sacrifice of prayer and intercession at all times and for all believers!

PAUL'S REQUEST FOR PRAYER

And for me, that utterance may be given to me, that I may open my mouth boldly to make known the mystery of the gospel… that in it I may speak boldly, as I ought to speak.
—Ephesians 6:19–20

And for me"—what light these words cast on the deep reality of Paul's faith in the absolute necessity and the wonderful power of prayer! What did he ask the Ephesians to pray for? "*That utterance may be given to me, that I may open my mouth boldly…that in it I may speak boldly, as I ought to speak.*" By this time, Paul had been a minister of the Gospel for more than twenty years. One might think that he had such experience in preaching that it would come naturally to him to "*speak boldly, as [he] ought to speak.*" But so deep was his conviction of his own insufficiency and weakness, so absolute was his dependence on divine teaching and power, that he felt that he could not do the work as it should have been done without the direct help of God. The sense of his total and unalterable dependence on God, who was with him, teaching him what and how to speak, was the basis for all his confidence and the keynote of his whole life.

But there is more. In his twenty years of ministry, there were innumerable times when his circumstances were so bad that he was left to throw himself upon God alone, with no one to help him in prayer. And yet, such was his deep spiritual insight into the unity of the body of Christ, and into his own actual dependence on the prayers of others, that he pleaded with them to pray *"with all prayer and supplication in the Spirit, being watchful to this end with all perseverance and supplication"* (v. 18), and he asked them not to forget to pray for him. Just as a wrestler cannot afford to dispense with the help of the weakest members of his body in the struggle in which he is engaged, so Paul could not do without the prayers of the believers.

What a call to us in this twentieth century, to awake to the consciousness that Christ our Intercessor in heaven, and all believers here upon earth, are engaged in one mighty battle! It is our duty to call out and cultivate the gift of unceasing supplication for the power of God's Spirit in all His servants, so that all may be given divine utterance and all *"may speak boldly, as* [they] *ought to speak."*

115

PRAYER FOR ALL BELIEVERS

To the saints and faithful brethren in Christ who are in Colosse....We give thanks to God...praying always for you, since we heard of...your love for all the saints.
—Colossians 1:2–4

Continue earnestly in prayer, being vigilant in it with thanksgiving; meanwhile praying also for us.
—Colossians 4:2–3

Prayer for all believers—it will take much time, thought, and love to see all that is included in this simple expression. Think of your own neighborhood and the believers you know. Think of your whole country, and praise God for all who are His children. Think of all the Christian nations of the world, and the believers to be found in each of these. Think of all the unsaved nations and the children of God to be found among them in ever increasing numbers.

Think of all the different circumstances and conditions in which these are to be found, and all the varying needs that call for God's grace and help. Think of many—oh, so many—who are God's children, and yet through ignorance or sloth, through worldlymindedness or an evil heart of unbelief, are walking in the dark and are bringing no honor to God. Think of so many who are in earnest and yet are conscious of a life of failure, with little or no power to please God or to bless man. Then think again of those who are to be found everywhere, in solitary places or among company, whose one aim is to serve the Lord who bought them and to be the light of those around them. Think of them especially as joining, often unaware of their relationship to the whole body of Christ, in pleading for the great promise of the Holy Spirit and the love and oneness of heart that He alone can give.

This is not the work of one day or one night. It needs a heart that will set itself to do serious thinking in regard to the condition of the body of Christ to which we belong. But once we begin, we will find what abundant reason there is for our persevering and yielding to God's Spirit, so that He may prepare us for the great and blessed work of daily praying the twofold prayer: for the love of God and Christ to fill the hearts of His people, and for the power of the Holy Spirit to come down and accomplish God's work in this sinful world.

116

PRAYER BY ALL BELIEVERS

We trust that He will still deliver us,
you also helping together in prayer for us.
—2 Corinthians 1:10–11

[Some] preach Christ from selfish ambition…supposing to
add affliction to my chains.…For I know that this will turn
out for my deliverance through your prayer and the supply of
the Spirit of Jesus Christ.
—Philippians 1:16, 19

This subject calls us once again to think of all believers throughout the world, but leads us to view them from a different stand-
point. If we ask God to increase the number and the power of those
who do pray, we will be led to form some impression of the hope
that our circle of intercessors may gradually increase in number
and power.

Our first thoughts will naturally turn to the multitude of
believers who know very little about the duty or the blessedness
of pleading for the body of Christ, or for all the work that has to
be done to perfect its members. We then have to remember how
many people do intercede for the power of His Spirit—and we
thank God for them—but whose thoughts are chiefly limited to
spheres of work with which they are acquainted or in which they
are directly interested.

That leaves us with what is, comparatively speaking, a very limited number of people who will be ready to take part in the prayer that ought to be sent up by the whole church for the unity of the body and the power of the Spirit. And even then, the number may be small who really feel drawn to take part in this daily prayer for the outpouring of the Spirit on all God's people.

And yet many may be feeling that the proposal meets a long-felt need, and that it is an unspeakable privilege, whether with few or many, to make Christ's last prayer, *"That they may be one"* (John 17:11), the daily supplication of our faith and love. In time, believers might join together in small circles or throughout wider districts, helping to rouse those around them to take part in the great work of making prayer for all believers become one prayer prayed by all believers.

This message is sent out to all who desire to be in touch with it and who seek to prove their consecration to their Lord in the unceasing, daily supplication for the power of His love and Spirit to be revealed to all His people.

117

PRAYER FOR ALL THE FULLNESS OF THE SPIRIT

"Bring all the tithes into the storehouse…and try Me now in this," says the LORD of hosts, "if I will not open for you the windows of heaven and pour out for you such blessing that there will not be room enough to receive it."
—Malachi 3:10

This last promise in the Old Testament tells us how abundant the blessing is to be. Pentecost was only the beginning of what God is willing to do. The promise of the Father, as Christ presented it, still waits for its perfect fulfillment. Let us try to realize the liberty that we possess to ask and expect great things.

Just as the great command to *"go…and preach the gospel"* (Mark 16:15) was meant not only for the disciples, but also for us, so the very last command—*"Tarry…until you are endued with power from on high"* (Luke 24:49); *"Wait for the Promise of the Father….You shall be baptized with the Holy Spirit"* (Acts 1:4–5)—is also for us and is the basis for the confident assurance that our prayers with one accord will be heard.

Take time to think of the cry of need that can be heard throughout the whole church and throughout all our mission fields. Let us realize that the only remedy that can be found for ineffectiveness or powerlessness, to enable us to gain the victory over the powers of this world and of darkness, is in the manifested presence of our Lord in the midst of His hosts and in the power of His Spirit. Let us take time to think of the state of all the churches throughout Christendom, until we are brought deeper than ever to believe that nothing except the supernatural, almighty intervention of our Lord Himself will rouse His hosts for the great battle against evil. Can anyone imagine or suggest any other matter for prayer that can compete with this: for the power of God on the ministers of the Gospel, and on all His people, to fill them *"with power from on high"* (Luke 24:49) that will make the Gospel the power of God unto salvation?

As we connect the prayer for the whole church on earth with the prayer for the whole power of God in heaven, we will feel that the greatest truths of the heavenly world and the kingdom of God have possession of us, and that we are indeed asking what God is longing to give, as soon as He finds hearts utterly yielded to Him in faith and obedience.

EVERY DAY

Give us day by day our daily bread.
—Luke 11:3

Some Christians are afraid that a promise to pray every day is altogether beyond them. They could not undertake it, and yet they pray to God to give them their bread "*day by day.*" Surely if a child of God has once yielded himself with his whole life to God's love and service, he should consider it a privilege to take advantage of any invitation that would help him every day to come into God's presence with the great need of His church and kingdom.

Many confess that they desire to live wholly for God. They acknowledge that Christ gave Himself for them and that His love now watches over them and works in them without ceasing. They acknowledge the claim that nothing less than the measure of Christ's love for us is to be the measure of our love for Him. They feel that if this is indeed to be the standard of their lives, they surely ought to welcome every opportunity for proving each day that they are devoting their hearts' strength to the interests of Christ's kingdom and to the prayer that can bring down God's blessings.

Our invitation to daily, united prayer may come to some as a new and perhaps unexpected opportunity of becoming God's remembrancers who "*cry out day and night*" (Luke 18:7) for His power and blessing on His people and on this needy world. Think of the privilege of being allowed to plead every day with God on behalf of His children, for the outpouring of His Spirit, and for the coming of His kingdom that His will may indeed be done on earth as it is in heaven (Matthew 6:10). To those who have to confess that they have scarcely understood the high privilege and the solemn duty of waiting on God in prayer for His blessing on the world, the invitation ought to be most welcome. And even to those who already have their special circles for which to pray, the thought that their vision and their hearts can be enlarged to include all God's children, all the work of His kingdom, and all the promise of an abundant outpouring of His Spirit, should urge them to take part in a ministry by which their other work will not suffer, but their hearts will be strengthened with a joy, a love, and a faith that they have never known before.

119

WITH ONE ACCORD

They were all with one accord in one place.…And they were all filled with the Holy Spirit.
—Acts 2:1, 4

Several of the previous chapters have opened to us wonderful thoughts of the unity of the whole body of Christ, and the need for deliberately cultivating the slumbering or buried talents of intercession. We may indeed thank God, for we know of the tens of thousands of His children who in daily prayer are pleading for some portion of the work of God's kingdom in which they are personally interested. But in many cases in which they take an interest, there is a lack of the largehearted and universal love that embraces all the children of God and their service. The people do not have the boldness and strength that come from the consciousness of being part of a large and conquering army under the leadership of our conquering King.

I have said that a wrestler must gather up all his strength and depend on every member of his body to do its very utmost. In an army with millions of soldiers at war, each detachment not only throws its whole heart into the work that it has to do, but it is also ready to rejoice and take new courage from every report of bravery and enthusiasm of the fardistant members of the same army. Is this not what we need in the church of Christ—such an enthusiasm for the King and His kingdom that His name will be made known to every human being? Do we not need such a faith in His purpose that our prayers will rise up every day with a largehearted love that grasps the whole body of Christ and pleads daily for the power of the Holy Spirit on all its members, even to the very weakest?

The strength that unity gives is something inconceivable. The power of each individual member is increased greatly by the inspiration of fellowshipping with a large and conquering multitude. Nothing can so help believers to an ever larger faith as the consciousness of being one body and one spirit in Christ Jesus. Only as the disciples were all *"with one accord in one place"* on the Day of Pentecost *"were* [they] *all filled with the Holy Spirit."* United prayer brings the answer to prayer.

120

A PERSONAL CALL

*We should not trust in ourselves but in God…who delivered
us…and…will still deliver us.*
—2 Corinthians 1:9–10

*[Some] preach Christ from selfish ambition…
supposing to add affliction to my chains.…For I know that
this will turn out for my deliverance through your prayer and
the supply of the Spirit of Jesus Christ.*
—Philippians 1:16, 19

Scriptures like these prove that there were still Christians in the churches under the full power of the Holy Spirit, on whom Paul could depend for *"effective, fervent prayer"* (James 5:16). When we plead with Christians to *"pray without ceasing"* (1 Thessalonians 5:17), there are many who quietly decide that such a life is not possible for them. They do not have any special gift for prayer; they do not have that intense desire for glorifying Christ in the salvation of souls; they have not yet learned what it is, under the power of the love of Christ, to live not for themselves, but for Him who died for them and rose again (2 Corinthians 5:15).

And yet we bring to them the call to offer themselves in wholehearted surrender to live entirely for Christ. We ask them whether they are not ashamed of the selfish life that simply uses Christ as a convenience to escape from hell and to secure a place in heaven. We come to them with the assurance that God can change their lives and fill their hearts with Christ and His Holy Spirit. We plead with them to believe that *"with God all things are possible"* (Matthew 19:26). He is able and willing; He is anxious to restore them to the Father's house, to the joy of His presence and service.

In order to attain this, they must listen to the call for men and women who will daily and continually, in the power of Christ's abiding presence, live in the spirit of unceasing intercession for all believers. They must receive the power of the Holy Spirit and acknowledge that this is nothing less than a duty, a sacrifice that Christ's love has a right to claim, and that He by His Spirit will indeed work in them. The person who accepts the call as coming from Christ and draws near to God in humble prayer for the needed grace, however far he may have come short, will have taken the first step on the path that leads to fellowship with God, to a new faith and life in Christ Jesus, and to the surrender of his whole being to the intercession of the Spirit that will help to bring Pentecost again into the hearts of God's people.

ABOUT THE AUTHOR

Andrew Murray (1828–1917) was an amazingly prolific Christian writer who lived and ministered as both a pastor and author in the towns and villages of South Africa. Some of Murray's earliest works were an extension of his pastoral work, written to provide nurture and guidance to Christians, whether young or old in the faith. Once books such as *Abide in Christ, Divine Healing,* and *With Christ in the School of Prayer* were written, Murray became widely known, and new books from his pen were awaited with great eagerness around the world.

He wrote to give daily practical help to many of the people in his congregation who lived out in the farming communities and could come into town for church services only on rare occasions. As he wrote these books of instruction, Murray adopted the practice of placing many of his more devotional books into thirty-one separate readings to correspond with the days of the month.

At the age of seventy-eight, Murray resigned from the pastorate and devoted most of his time to his manuscripts. He continued to write profusely, moving from one book to the next with an intensity of purpose and a zeal that few men of God have ever equaled. He often said of himself, rather humorously, that he was like a hen about to hatch an egg; he was restless and unhappy until he got the burden of the message off his mind.

During these later years, after hearing of pocket-sized paperbacks, Murray immediately began to write books to be published in that fashion. He thought it was a splendid way to have the teachings of the Christian life at your fingertips, where they could be carried around and read at any time of the day.

Murray's writings still move the emotions, search the conscience, and reveal the sins and shortcomings of many of us with a love and hope born out of an intimate knowledge of the mercy and faithfulness of God.

Countless people have hailed Andrew Murray as their spiritual father and given credit for much of their Christian growth to the influence of his devotional books.

Welcome to Our House!

We Have a Special Gift for You ...

It is our privilege and pleasure to share in your love of Christian classics by publishing books that enrich your life and encourage your faith.

To show our appreciation, we invite you to sign up to receive a specially selected **Reader Appreciation Gift**, with our compliments. Just go to the Web address at the bottom of this page.

God bless you as you seek a deeper walk with Him!

WE HAVE A GIFT FOR YOU

whpub.me/classicthx

WHITAKER HOUSE